M000303700

TESTED

A New Strategy for
KEEPING KIDS IN THE FAITH

Information about the *TESTED is Trained* series of teachings and Brace E. Barber's availability for speaking and training can be found at www.BraceBarber.com.

Join us for insights, discussion and community at https://www.facebook.com/bracebarberauthor/

Other works by Brace E. Barber
- *RANGER SCHOOL, No Excuse Leadership* (Patrol Leader Press 2000) www.RangerSchool.com
- *NO EXCUSE LEADERSHIP; Lessons from the U.S. Army's Elite Rangers* (J. Wiley and Sons 2003) www.NoExcuseLeadership.com
- *Sun Tzu's PATTERN of POWER; The Art of War Organized for Decision Making* (Patrol Leader Press 2011, 2016)

Brace E. Barber

Dedication
My wife and I dedicate this book to our children, Brace, Ethan and Sophia. They are the reason this mission to prepare kids to battle the world took on urgency several years ago. We pray that we have been good stewards of them as God's children. Each of them has provided invaluable insights to us. Through their feedback, they have challenged us to teach them more effectively. They have endured the years of teaching, testing and questioning that have accompanied our enthusiastic embrace of the evidence God has provided in support the reliability of His Word.

Acknowledgements

My wife, Natasha, is my biggest encourager. She is also my toughest sounding board. I have a tendency to fall in love with my *perfect* ideas. She has a way of lovingly letting me know that some of them are not so perfect. She has refined me and focused me more times that I can count and she has been my partner in forming this book. I am exceedingly grateful to God for her.

In any long-term endeavor like this there are countless people who have contributed and participated. Loren Ware provided the conversation that God used to convicted me of the importance of the task. Mark Campbell took time to provide expert guidance on what and how to attack the problem. Steve King and Mark Millard expended great amounts of imagination and energy in helping me with messaging and my introductory video. Hoyt Condra, Jason Carson, Paul Wilkinson and Wes Sellers provided some great perspective as did Todd and Cindy Parish, and John Leech. Ben and Allison Calhoun, Warwick and Tanya Burns and many others provided candid input on my *perfect* design ideas. Tom and Leighann McCoy took their time to review my material and provided invaluable feedback. Jason Ellerbrook and Maurice Painter have been enthusiastic about the project and about supporting it in the market.

TESTED; A New Strategy for KEEPING KIDS IN THE FAITH

Table of Contents

Perspective

I asked my 8th grade Sunday-school class recently, "How do you become a Christian?" Their answers showed a surprising lack of knowledge of basic Christian doctrine. Some of their answers mentioned Jesus, but most said something to the effect, "Believe in God." These kids weren't the non-churched friends of the regulars invited for a special doughnut-day at church. These were the regulars.

They are smart kids raised by Bible-believing parents in a Bible-teaching Baptist Church in middle Tennessee. In terms of the US faith demographics, this may as well be a suburb of where Jesus grew up. Though Christian illiteracy is common and troublesome, the process of uncovering it gives us the power to overcome it.

The simple act of asking a specific question and getting answers from kids gives us a world of insight into their education level and understanding. Their answers give us knowledge of the subjects on which we need to focus our time in teaching the faith. More importantly, we cannot just talk about the subjects; we must continue to test their knowledge of the subjects.

We do not measure kids' knowledge or beliefs and so we are surprised when they walk out never to return

In this book I focus on how to best prepare our kids for the future battle in the world so that they stay in the faith.[1] One of the two foundational premises on which this strategy rests is that by testing kids' knowledge of what we teach, we have the ability to know what they know. By knowing what they know and just as importantly, what they don't know, we can adjust our teaching and our topics to make sure that they learn what we want them to learn – what they must learn.

The simplicity and power of such an exercise cannot be overstated. The problem, as you will discover, is that the Church, big-C, is shocked by the exodus of kids from the faith when they leave high school. We simply do not ask, we do not test, we do not measure kids' knowledge or beliefs and so we are surprised when they walk out never to return. Week after week we teach kids, never knowing that deep skepticism is growing within in the majority of them. I call this the disease of skepticitis.

Skepticitis is a cancer of skepticism about the truth of Christianity, which if not treated is deadly. Seventy five percent (75%) of kids raised in Christian homes are already succumbing to the disease. Quite often the disease has no symptoms until the child reaches the age of 18, at which point they reveal a deep-rooted disbelief in Christianity. The sufferer often projects anger and mocks the faith and those who practice

---

[1] This book is focused on the kids raised in Christian homes or who regularly attend church or Sunday school. I am making no claims about the state of salvation of the kids through high school. The theology of *once saved always saved* and *apostasy* remain untouched by this work. The point of this work is to prepare kids raised in Christian homes and those who fill church youth groups prosper in their Christian faith after they leave home.

it. Every child raised in a Christian home is susceptible to skepticitis and should be proactively treated.

Ken Ham, in his book, *Already Gone, Why Your Kids Will Quit Church and What You Can Do to Stop it,* says, "A spiritual black plague has almost killed the next generation of European believers. ..., and now the same disease is infecting North America."[2] I believe that preventative care can protect the majority of pre-high school graduates. However, once a person suffers from skepticitis it is possible, but very difficult to overcome the disease. These sufferers may live without the hope of salvation and God's peace for the rest of their lives and into eternity.

The treatment for skepticitis is the proper teaching of the Full Testimony of God and the testing of the student's knowledge. The Full Testimony of God includes the Scriptures and all of the evidence God provided that supports the Scriptures. Partial testimony and ineffective measuring processes are responsible for the massive numbers of Christian kids lost to the disease. Churches that only teach the gospel and Biblical perspectives without the supporting evidence and without measuring progress suffer a 75% loss.

The treatment for skepticitis is (1) the proper teaching of the Full Testimony of God and (2) the testing of the student's knowledge.

---

[2] Already Gone, Why Your Kids Will Quit Church and What You Can Do to Stop it, by Ken Ham and Britt Beemer, Published by Master Books, 2009

In this book parents and churches will learn how to work to cure skepticitis and increase the chances of keeping kids in the faith. You will learn the step by step method for properly teaching the Full Testimony of God and how it effectively treats the disease. The objective of this book is to give churches and parents the tools to produce Scripture-following Christians who live out their faith and fulfill the Great Commission.

As we dive into curing skepticitis, we must face the truth of the disease. The Church's attempt to be relevant to today's youth has focused more and more on relationships rather than even the gospel; on experience rather than knowledge of God. The Barna Group conducted extensive research that showed the importance of relationships and adult mentorship in the lives of the kids who *remain* in the church. However, David Kinnaman, President of the Barna Group, highlighted the limitations of such a study when he said, "It's important for anyone who uses research to realize correlation does not equal causation."[3]

There is a major distinction between the things that we find in the lives of kids who *stay* in the church and the reasons why kids *leave* the church. What David Kinnaman is saying is that just because kids who stay in the church have close relationships and good mentors does not mean that those are the reasons why they stay. Furthermore, the lack of strong relationships does not mean that a person will leave. Therefore, in order to truly address the problem of kids leaving the church, we first have to identify why the kids are *leaving*. At the same time, we must change our perspective to understand that there

---

[3] 5 Reasons Millennials Stay Connected to Church, September 17, 2013
https://www.barna.com/research/5-reasons-millennials-stay-connected-to-church/

is a large portion of our kids that we teach every week who have already left. Their decision to leave is not a post-high school decision.

The objective of this book is to give churches and parents the tools to produce Scripture-following Christians who live out their faith and fulfill the Great Commission

---

The book, *Already Gone*, found that of those kids who leave the church, 39.8% first had doubts about the truth of the stories in the Bible while they were in middle school, while 43.7% first had doubts in high school. Only 10.6% first doubted in college.[4] When was the last time you provided any evidence for the truthfulness of any story in the Bible that would answer common doubts? When was the last time that you tested their knowledge about that evidence?

We can separate the kids in our Sunday school classes into two categories; kids who will remain in the faith and kids who will leave the faith. Unfortunately, under today's teaching processes we can't tell which is which until they wander away after high school. Even testing will only go part of the way to identifying kids at risk of leaving. The best we can do is to formulate a strategy to apply to the entire group that encourages the largest portion of those kids to remain in the Christian Church into adulthood.

---

[4] Already Gone, Why Your Kids Will Quit Church and What You Can Do to Stop it, by Ken Ham and Britt Beemer, Published by Master Books, 2009

As unrealistic as it is, I propose that we set as a goal saving 100% of the kids we see on Sunday mornings. If we believe that we have exhausted our options and that the world is overcoming the Church, then we have forfeited the game while we are still well positioned to win. Jesus gave us a clear idea of his priorities when he said, *"What do you think? If a man owns a hundred sheep, and one of them wanders away, will he not leave the ninety-nine on the hills and go to look for the one that wandered off? (Matthew 18:12).*

Amazingly, the Christian Church has 75 sheep that have wandered off without us knowing. We thought we were tending the entire flock while we were really only feeding and watering 25 of them. Our challenge then is to figure out how to go after the 75 without abandoning the 25.

If we continue to structure our teaching and youth events around the reasons kids *stay* in the Church, we are choosing to let the other 75 sheep get lost in the hills. Fortunately, there is good reason for optimism. The methods we use now for retaining the 25 are perfectly compatible with what I propose are the methods for retaining the majority of the 75 who are at risk of wandering off. We should develop close relationships, engage adult mentors, go on mission trips, perform acts of service, teach the Gospel of Christ and teach how to live Godly lives in a secular world.

We should also teach the rest of the Full Testimony of God in order to evidentially support the foundation of our beliefs. The evidence for the reliability of the Word of God and the stories found within it will deepen kids' belief and strengthen the bonds that they build with each other. These methods work together.

Secular Education and Relationships

We must recognize that in all we do, we are competing with the secular world. We are competing with secular relationships and education. We are attempting to develop relationships and educate the kids in a couple hours a week while their friends, schools, sports teams, TV, the internet and social media have the kids for the rest of the time. With regards to time, we are outnumbered 50 to 1. That disadvantage is especially important in our ability to develop stronger relationships with them in the Church than they have outside of the Church. It simply takes time to develop trust and comfort with another person, and secular friends and relationships have us surrounded.

We must provide a place where kids are welcome and where they feel that they belong. We must do our very best to create personal bonds with our kids in order to allow for faith to be an attractive option to the self-centered secular world in which they are immersed for the vast majority of the week. However, a strategy revolving around relationships is predictably in trouble if the goal is to keep kids in the faith.

While the secular world has much more time to educate our kids than we do, the playing field will be much more even if we educate our kids properly during the short time that we have them. We know that the world is doing everything it can to undermine the legitimacy of the Christian Church, its beliefs and its source. Secular education does not just attack Jesus, it has endless targets from the Judeo-Christian Scriptures as well.

Secular education attacks the *scientific* impossibility of creation, of designed life, of God-inspired Scripture to the point where their positions are simply accepted facts. Currently, the Church does very little to refute that secular education. The Church does plenty to explain its views and how to live in accordance with them, but it does almost nothing to explain why we should believe in the reliability of the source of our beliefs. This condition has left the secular world unchallenged and has severely damaged the faith of our kids.

What I propose is that evidence is independent of time and that facts are timeless. We can use our one hour per week to overcome the 50 hours of secular influence. A set of facts which support a certain claim can be presented in 30 minutes and it can affect the beliefs and behaviors of a person for a lifetime. Of course, this works just as well for Christian and non-Christian beliefs alike and it is the person hearing the evidence who gets to judge which is most convincing. In this environment where a short amount of time can mean the difference between belief and disbelief, the Church has an enormous opportunity to save our children. The key to using that time effectively is in what information we give and how well we ensure it is understood.

A set of facts which support a certain claim can be presented in 30 minutes and it can affect the beliefs and behaviors of a person for a lifetime

13

If the Church had been providing the right kind of information for the past 40 years, we would not have the systemic loss of kids from the Church that we have today. The right information is that which presents the Scripture, the Gospel of Jesus Christ and all of the evidence supporting those beliefs. The right information in context of the battle for the minds of our kids is to refute the world's evidence and promote positive evidence to back up our claims.

Think of it this way. The Church and the world are trying to get your kids to buy their car.

The world says, "The Church's car does not have an engine."

The Church responds, "Look at the pretty paint job."

The world persists in pointing at the hood, hour after hour, day after day, "Their engine is a fantasy."

And the Church persists, "Wait until we get the car detailed."

Which side are your kids going to believe?

The Church is not exposing its engine, only its paint job. We are making the car a comfortable place to sit, but not giving us any evidence that it will run. It's easy to describe the paint job, but it takes work to explain the engine. I propose that we throw open the hood and expose the incredible, powerful, eternal engine of the Church. When our kids understand that the evidence from every field of science, history and philosophy overwhelmingly support the Christian worldview, they will rev the engine. They will take it onto the street and idle proudly at a stop light next to the secular car. Then, when the light turns green, the secular car will sit there making the clicking sound of a dead battery as our kids drive way. *That's* when the secular driver exclaims, "Well, it's just arrogant to think that you know for sure that your car has an engine." Once a student understands the strong evidence supporting the reliability of Scriptures, the battle for their faith gets a lot easier. When a kid can understand that science has shown that the Universe came from nothing just like the Bible says, it dulls the secular analysis surrounding that topic. When the astounding improbability of the Theory of Evolution is exposed, and the amazing evidence of design is presented, kids are less likely to buy into the atheist view of reality. And when the Resurrection of Christ can be presented as the only reasonable explanation for the accepted facts of the event surrounding Christ's death, the cornerstone to their own faith is set in place.

Though the world has much more time with our kids, we have the advantage of truth. It is my opinion that truth matters more than relationships, and it is the truth that our kids are seeking. Relationships can support the truth, but truth saves, not relationships with other people. The truth does not change, but relationships often do. If a student is convinced beyond a reasonable doubt that Jesus is the Christ, then they will want a relationship with Him, and that is the most important relationship. They will endure hypocritical and damaging Christian relationships better than if they are counting on Christians to always reflect Christ.

Relationships are important, but not between teacher and student. Who has a close relationship with their pastor? A church does not have to be very big before a pastor loses the ability to have a close relationship with every person in his congregation. Does that affect his ability to teach? I'd suggest that every church with more than 20 people is evidence that lack of a personal relationship with each person does not diminish a pastor's ability to effectively teach. In the same way, youth Sunday-school teachers do not have to have a close relationship with their students in order to effectively teach the truth. What matters is that the student believes the information that the teacher is presenting. If relationships were critical in the teacher-student equation, then no book would hold value, no Church would grow past a few couples and no student curriculum could gain popularity. All sources of information would have to be transmitted from one close friend to another. Truth transcends relationships.

My purpose is to give churches and parents the tools to teach youth beyond a reasonable doubt that Jesus is the Christ, that the Scriptures are reliable as well as a whole lot more. Relationships will flourish in the process.

Educational Emphasis

I believe that Christian parents and Churches are facing an intellectual battle to which they have not yet adjusted. We have not adjusted our education methods to address the serious challenge posed by the secular education system. The secular world uses a process of education that includes teaching, testing and reinforcement. We as Christian parents demand that our educators make sure our kids learn the information they are teaching. We send our kids to school five days a week, make them do homework and want them to take their education seriously. We demand that our kids learn what is taught regardless of the sacrifices, after all, "You want to get a good job, don't you?"

The Church, in contrast, is presenting information that is far more valuable to a person's eternity than anything taught in school. In fact, the Church is teaching truths that will make people's lives here on earth more peaceful and fulfilling no matter their station in life, and yet parents treat the Church's educational system with a small fraction of the urgency and importance they give secular education.

Certainly parents force their kids to get up for church every Sunday, but that's not the sacrifice I am talking about. Where are your kids' last Sunday-school handouts? How much time did you spend with them learning those lessons during the week? If you are like us, you ask the kids about their time in class on the way home or to the restaurant. If they took a handout from the class, which is rare, it was quickly discarded at home. Though the subject matter may have been wonderful, our attention to the topic was complete after a short discussion. There was no testing or reinforcement.

The point is not that we should be pouring a whole bunch of academic requirements on our kids, but that we should be treating their Christian education as a priority. We as parents, working with the Church, should be seeking ways to keep our kids in the faith. We should be doing whatever is necessary to give our kids the best chance at salvation, which is far more important than reading, writing and arithmetic.

Has someone ever handed you a box that you thought was empty but as soon as you took it realized it was full? Despite

17

your surprise, you didn't let the box drop; rather you instantly added more muscle to keep the box steady. This is the difference in perspective I'm trying to relay. We are acting as if we are passing around empty boxes while 75% of them are crashing on the floor and we are oblivious to it. Helping lift our kids to salvation is a much heavier job than we understand.

Here's the situation in which we find ourselves:

- Approximately 75% of kids raised in Christian homes leave the faith after high school. Multiple studies over the past 15 years confirm the massive loss of kids.

- These kids tell us that the main reasons they leave revolve around the lack of evidence for the Christian worldview. In their minds, scientific, historic and logical truths contradict the Bible.

- The people who have led the youth groups and churches over the past generation are the same ones developing 'strategies' and curriculum for this generation.

- The methods illustrated in this book directly address the reasons that kids are leaving the Christian faith in order to remove those justifications.

Truth transcends relationships

If Satan were devising a plan to destroy the Christian Church, he would eliminate any awareness of the necessity of preparing our youth to withstand the false teachings of the culture he has been cultivating. He would have the Church avoid answering the hard questions for our kids. He would segregate Christianity to a place where Christians speak their own language, unintelligible to the secular world. He would convince them that it is hopeless to look at scientific and historic evidence for support of their faith. He would direct them towards teaching methods that fail to prepare their children to understand their own faith. He would build a Christian culture that believes that it must intellectually coddle youth and expect no exertion from them. He would foster skepticitis. Ultimately this devious plan would result in 75% of kids raised in Christian homes leaving the faith after high school.

On the other hand, what plan would the Christian Church make to energize its followers and impact the world?

- ✓ Expect our youth to learn the core tenants of its faith and make sure they know it.
- ✓ Teach its youth the Word of God.
- ✓ Prepare its youth to withstand the false teachings of the secular culture.
- ✓ Teach Christians the scientific and historic evidence supporting the faith and make sure they know it.
- ✓ Teach Christians to persuasively communicate truth in the cultural language of science, history and philosophy.
- ✓ Train Christians to lovingly grapple with people in the world so that we can bring them to a saving knowledge of Christ.
- ✓ Build relationships within the Church.

✓ Provide opportunities to serve the Church and
community.

✓ Underlie everything we do with gentleness and respect
with the goal of saving lost souls.

If we are going to prepare our youth to impact the world then
we must train them. We will have to guide our kids through
exercises combating secular ideas. When was the last time
anyone addressed the skeptic's claims of the 'truth' of
evolution or the 'evilness' of God in their classroom? If we
were training our kids to take on the world, then these are basic
activities that we would do – routinely. The process proposed
in this book will allow every parent, group and church to easily
and effectively deal with these subjects. This book will take
you through the very first steps to achieving great results with
your youth. As your youth become strengthened in their
knowledge and faith, there are opportunities to train them how
to effectively engage the world.

Has anyone invited an atheist into their classroom to have a
conversation about their perspectives and why they believe
Christianity to be false? Though this level of engagement is a
valuable type of training and beyond the scope of this book, I
do feel that it is important to introduce you to this idea as part
of this Perspective section. Just the idea of exposing our kids to
a real-life atheist requires a lot of thought and contemplation.
Will this person convince my child that Christianity is false?
Will they provide facts that I cannot combat and which will
take my child down a path towards leaving the Church? Have I
done enough to prepare my kids for the experience?

I invited an atheist to present to my high-school apologetics class and engage in a discussion. The parents of one of the students pulled their child from the class for the day, while the other 10 students and most of their parents participated. The students were engaged, and our guest was respectful. Though every encounter will be different, the students were struck by the lack of answers that our guest had for the meaning of life, the origin of life and the beginning of the Universe. The faith and confidence of these kids was greatly strengthened as was their confidence in engaging the world. Is an atheist encounter like this far beyond the scope of possibilities for your group? It does not have to be.

Evaluate why we don't proactively plan engagements like this for our kids while we can guide them. We know that after high school our kids will be in constant engagement with foreign beliefs where we can't guide them. We are uncomfortable having controlled engagements like this, but we don't think twice about sending kids alone into a hostile world filled with people who will pick apart their beliefs.

Safe, guided interactions with different worldviews prior to graduating high school looks like this.

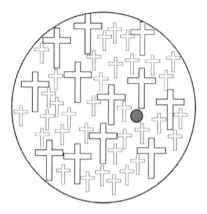

Eventual exposure to other worldviews in unsafe, unprotected environments when kids have not been prepared to combat false ideas looks like this.

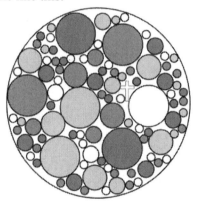

When kids have the education and training to bring truth to the world, then they impact the world for Christ.

The methods of teaching and the subject matter I propose are designed to place the unavoidable truth for the Christian worldview in the path of our students. My purpose is to allow churches to face students with the scientific and historic truth for Christianity that they must deal with as they are evaluating their faith decision. Though we cannot force salvation onto them, we can make sure that they know the truth even if they choose to leave the faith.

Intellectual doubts underlie the majority of reasons why kids leave the Church and why most that stay are timid. We can remove the intellectual barriers to accepting Jesus Christ as their Savior and prepare them for confident engagement with the world. Skepticitis is a curable disease.

Download multiple *TESTED is Trained* formatted teaching series at the Resource section of www.BraceBarber.com.

Chapter 1: Strategy Development

Take this **Pre-Test** prior to reading the chapter. Yes. There is a purpose behind answering these questions which will become clear as you read the book. You will get the most out of the book if you take the short moment to do the exercise.

	Question	Pre-test		Post-test	
1	Church teaching methods have been effective in retaining youth in the Christian faith.	T	F	T	F
2	A seminary degree and ten years or more experience as a pastor/youth pastor should be required to develop curriculum.	T	F	T	F
3	The Church does not know why youth leave the Church after high school.	T	F	T	F

Direction to Salvation

On October, 13 1972, a flight carrying 45 people crashed into the frozen, desolate heights of the Andes Mountains. The pilot died, leaving the co-pilot as the best authority on their location. He said that they were located much closer to civilization towards the west than they actually were.

When the survivors sent a small expedition to find rescuers, the party headed west on what they expected would be a tough but relatively short journey. What they found was a horizon filled with snow-covered mountains. The trek took 10 days before the two travelers were able to reach the edges of civilization and get word to rescuers. Only 16 of the 45 people survived the 72-day ordeal and all of them had to resort to cannibalism in order to live. All of the survivors suffered from some form of physical ailment including altitude sickness, dehydration, frostbite, broken bones, scurvy and malnutrition.

When we compare the survival rate of the passengers on this plane to the rate of youth raised in the Church who survive to be Christian adults, we find nearly the same percentage. Over 65% of kids raised in Christian homes leave the Christian church after high school. Research has returned numbers as high as 87.5% of kids leaving the faith. The majority of those that remain suffer from some sort theological malnutrition.

On August 24, 2016 the Pew Research Center published some findings from their ongoing study of the Religious Landscape of the United States. Their findings are consistent with every other study that has been conducted over the past 15 years. "Perhaps the most striking trend in American religion in recent years has been the growing percentage of adults who do not identify with a religious group. The vast majority of these religious "nones" (78%) say they were raised as a member of a particular religion before shedding their religious identity in adulthood. "About half of current religious "nones" who were raised in a religion (49%) indicate that a lack of belief led them to move away from religion. This includes many respondents who mention "science" as the reason they do not believe in religious teachings, including one who said "I'm a scientist now," and "I don't believe in miracles." Others reference "common sense," "logic" or a "lack of evidence" – or simply say they do not believe in God." "Eighteen percent say they are religiously unsure." [5]

The Church may never regain those who have already left the faith, but we do have the ability to work to save those youth still under our care. This book attempts to provide a path to survival for our Churches and kids. The purpose of this book and my ministry is to keep kids raised in Christian homes in the faith.

The survivors of the plane crash learned later that an abandoned hotel was only a two-day walk, downhill in the opposite direction. The closest town was an additional two-day walk along a downhill-sloping river valley.

---

[5] Why America's 'nones' left religion behind by Michael Lipka August 24, 2016 Pew Research Center. http://www.pewresearch.org/fact-tank/2016/08/24/why-americas-nones-left-religion-behind/

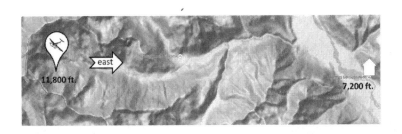

There is no guarantee that the survivors would have been rescued earlier or even survived had they gone to the east, but if the co-pilot had known where they were, the expedition would have certainly gone that direction. The way they went to the west was uphill while the way east was downhill; not by just a little bit, a lot. The westward expedition had to climb over 3,000 feet to about 15,000 feet before descending into a maze of mountains and valleys for the next week. This is a height greater than the tallest mountain in the continental US. To the east the expedition would have descended quickly to 9,000 feet where the air was thicker and temperatures were warmer. The valley to the east would have funneled the travelers into a wide river valley and right into an abandoned hotel and hot springs at an altitude of about 7,200 feet. There were rooms in the hotel that would protect them from the environment, vegetation that could be burned for heat and for signaling, and fish in the river for food.

No one is blaming the pilot for being disoriented or the survivors for listening to him. In hindsight, however, why would they listen to a pilot who had just run into a mountaintop because he didn't know where he was? That aside, he was probably the best authority in the situation. But he was wrong, and it was a costly lack of accuracy. What if a geologist had been on the flight, someone who had travelled the mountains for years and was able to offer an alternative opinion of their location and suggest a different course of action? Would someone with experience on the ground be more valuable than someone whose experience is in the air?

Strategy Development

The Church needs people who are experienced navigating on the ground. The ground in this scenario is an expertise in strategic planning, not theology. The Church needs coaches who can clearly identify where the Church is in relation to the terrain and civilization. These are people who understand how to define an objective and plan a course of action taking every aspect of the situation into consideration. Strategists create plans based on actual conditions, and work diligently to turn every assumption into a fact. Strategists know that dealing with the truth of a situation, whether good or bad, is the first key to achieving success. Trained strategists will look at parents, pastors and youth pastors as key leaders with specific strengths and capabilities, and plan their roles in the larger scheme appropriately.

We are on the field of battle where parents and Churches are attempting to guide young church goers through the secular mountains to a point of civilization – salvation. The battle, which is already raging, pits major worldviews against each other. This is happening in the main arena; it is the decisive engagement; the contest where every side expends their last energies – forever. And to be clear, the Church is losing right now. The Church needs a coherent strategy to win, not old curriculum repackaged and labeled, "Strategy."

We as a Church have the benefit of looking back over the past generation to see what has worked and what hasn't worked. We look around and the situation is getting worse. We are losing more and more youth every year with no solution in sight. We continue to go up hill to the west with only minor changes in direction. Over the past generation, we have changed almost nothing except the titles to the curriculum, the lyrics of the songs and the styles of the clothes. We continue to try to be relevant to the kids in the same ways and the results are the same.

Here's my point, we have a lot of highly experienced people with lots of seminary education and church leadership experience and over the past generation, despite their best efforts, we have lost the majority of our kids to the world. And yet, we continue to go in approximately the same direction in hopes that little changes will make a big difference. My contention is that we will not overcome our problem utilizing the same methods that perpetuated the problem to begin with. We must have a new strategy. Let's go east!

Signs

Fortunately, we have a great set of studies that have been conducted over the past 15 years which identify why kids raised in Christian homes leave the Church after high school. These studies act as gigantic signs telling us how to turn our kids from the wrong direction. The Christian Church has crashed into the mountain and as we crawl

out from the wreckage we see large signs pointing us away from the hotel (Church). You will see that the studies do a wonderful job of identifying what we must overcome in order to save our kids. There is no easy path – let me repeat, there is no easy path – but there is hope in knowing that we can go the right direction.

Read the signs. Go a different direction. In order to go the right way, we will use methods that are well grounded in experience and success at every level of education. What if the school your kids go to did not test kids in any way? What if they were simply required to show up in each of their classes and listen to a lecture? What if they never had homework and never had to read anything? How much would they learn? How much would they know? How much would they be able to present to someone else? How much would they care?

Their retention would be a small fraction of what they retain as a result of the educational process that schools use now. Yet, our most dedicated youth groups and Sunday schools provide the equivalent of a lecture on Sunday mornings and Wednesday evenings. It is a rare occasion to expect a student to read something and take notes, let alone take a quiz. Reading and filling out notes is the type of effort usually associated with an extra-church Bible study. We never test students, and do not hold any of them accountable for knowing anything about a biblical worldview.

In order to head towards Church, we must enact different educational processes that overcome the reasons kids are leaving and which take us in the correct direction.

Socializing
Lecturing without measuring is socializing, it's not teaching. Socializing is not enough to prepare them for the battle that they will enter as young adults. Every youth group, no matter how energetic or large, that fails to measure the knowledge retained by its youth is simply socializing them. A popular verse for parents serious about raising their kids as Christians is Proverbs 22:6 KJV "6 Train up a child in the way he should go: and when he is old, he will not depart from it." The problem is that we are not training them, no matter how much we think that we are.

I have been a consumer of this method of teaching for the past 12 years as my kids have gone through the church system and as I teach the weekly lessons from whatever curriculum the Church leadership has chosen for that semester. But I'm not just a consumer; I'm a strategist, educated at West Point, trained in the military, experienced in the corporate world and an independent developer of strategic-planning processes. I see major flaws to our current strategy that is causing us to travel fruitlessly in the wrong direction. More than that, I'm the father of three teenaged kids and I have a mission to do everything that I can do to ensure that they develop a lifelong personal commitment to and relationship with Jesus Christ as their savior.

I cannot make that decision for them, but I can get them headed in the right direction so that they have the best chance possible of ending up where I want them to be with regard to salvation. The NIV version of that same verse, Proverbs 22:6 says, "Start children off on the way they should go, and even when they are old they will not turn from it." We need to start our children off to the east. That's what the signs are telling us.

Ephesians 6:4 NIV says, "Fathers, do not exasperate your children; instead, bring them up in the *training* and *instruction* of the Lord." (emphasis added) 2 Timothy 3:16-17 NIV says, "[16] All Scripture is God-breathed and is useful for *teaching*, rebuking, correcting and *training* in righteousness, [17] *so that* the servant of God may be *thoroughly equipped* for every good work." (emphasis added)

What good work?

The Great Commission

Matthew 28:19-20 NIV says, "[19] Therefore *go and make disciples* of all nations, baptizing them in the name of the Father and of the Son and of the Holy Spirit, [20] and *teaching* them to obey everything I have commanded you." (emphasis added)

Socialization is not teaching or training. Socialization is ineffective in thoroughly equipping our youth to go and make disciples. If there is a good argument against the effectiveness of expecting our kids to learn something and be tested on it, then I can't imagine what it is. R. C. Sproul said in his book, *Knowing Scripture,* "The Christian who is not diligently involved in the serious study of scripture is simply inadequate as a disciple of Christ. To be an adequate Christian, and competent in the things of God, we must do more than attend sharing sessions and bless me parties."[6] And though this book will have an apologetics, defending-the-faith prominence, the process I present is applicable for both Biblical and apologetics knowledge and it's critical to use for both sets of knowledge. I propose that this book guides you to the *more than* that R. C. Sproul suggests.

I give apologetics extra attention because the area is currently only an afterthought in churches. The subject areas are at best treated as an elective Bible study that people can do if they have an interest instead of an integrated component of God's message to the world and necessary to refute the claims of the world. The compartmentalizing of apologetics study is understandable in the sense that it does not conform easily to current Church educational process. Apologetics materials are detailed, academic and demand some level of education on the part of the teacher. Standard church curriculum today is much easier to teach because every man has been a boy and every woman has been a girl. We all have our own testimony and

---

[6] Knowing Scripture by R. C. Sproul published by IVP Books 2009

opinion on the subject being taught and can converse with kids on most biblical subjects without much preparation.

Even if we buy into the need for greater attention to apologetics instruction, how do we overcome the obstacles to teaching it?

Objectives of this Book

Here's what you will get out of this book:

- You will learn an approach for keeping kids in the faith
  - Learn how to give your children a much higher chance for remaining Christian even in the face of the secular world.
  - Learn how to support your church by helping students who need to be strengthened.
- Promise of this educational approach
  - Youth will be better equipped to fulfill the Great Commission.
  - Your youth will easily learn the evidence that supports the Christian worldview against the most aggressive secular attacks.
  - They will be able to converse with others of different opinions and use evidence to support their positions.
  - They will be able to be persuasive in the midst of a debate and set a Christian example for how to interact with the world in love.
- An identification of the problem.
  - You will learn about the hidden statistics showing the dramatic loss of kids from the Christian Church.

- o You will see that the loss of our youth is only a symptom of the real problem and why it has not been addressed by an effective strategy.
- o You will learn why our youth are the best place to focus to spark a revival in the entire Christian Church.
- An analysis of the causes of the real problem and who has responsibility to fix it
  - o You will learn to recognize the problem in your children and the youth group at church.
  - o You will learn why the youth are leaving the church.
  - o You will learn where the responsibility lies, what the real challenges are, and specifically why the solution must be designed in a more effective way.
- The design of the solution
  - o Allows laymen volunteers to teach apologetics and Bible subjects effectively. (The Full-Testimony of God)
  - o Requires limited preparation in line with what teachers currently have to do.
  - o Costs no money.
  - o Can be taught individually, with small groups and with very large groups.
  - o Can be conducted effectively in the short time you have the children each week.
- A step by step process for creating the solution for yourself and your children or youth group.

o You will learn how to prepare powerful lessons using free resources that cover every subject that you can imagine.

o You will learn the strategy behind each step of the lesson design and see for yourself how powerful it will be for your students.

Church Exit	Church
Believe in Science	Scientific Evidence
Miracles Impossible	Creation and Life
Jesus not God's Son	Fulfilled Prophecy
No Resurrection	Disciples' Martyrdom
All Faiths the Same	Contradictions
No Evidence	God's Full Testimony

Please Return to the Beginning of the Chapter and Take the Post-Test

Chapter 2: Strategy Overview

Take this Pre-Test prior to reading the chapter.

	Question	Pre-test		Post-test	
1	Once a person leaves the faith it is very difficult to get them to return.	T	F	T	F
2	Multiple studies provide clear reasons why Christian youth leave the faith.	T	F	T	F
3	Kids who stay are articulate about their Christian faith.	T	F	T	F
4	Most churches have clearly defined goals for what they want to accomplish with their youth	T	F	T	F
5	A greater emphasis on teaching Scripture will prepare youth for the challenges of this world.	T	F	T	F
6	I won't study apologetics because I have nothing to	T	F	T	F

	apologize for.				
7	Apologetics is a good side study but unnecessary for the Church body as a whole.	T	F	T	F
8	Our youth are the best source for starting a revival in America.	T	F	T	F

First Thanksgiving

The first Thanksgiving back home after leaving for college is really a special time. It rarely makes the front pages of life events, but when a young adult heads away from home to college, Thanksgiving is often the first time back home. Mine was a once-in-a-lifetime event. I left my home in El Cajon, California on my way to college in the complete opposite corner of America at West Point, New York. As it happened, West Point was playing Navy in a football game in Pasadena, California that year. It was the first and last time that the game was played there, and it required a huge movement of students all the way across the country. For me, it meant that West Point was going to deliver me home for Thanksgiving.

Though most coming-home-for-Thanksgiving trips are less involved, they are still a wonderful time to be together. The family gets a chance to spend time with their child learning about their experiences and plans for the future. Parents get to discover who their child is becoming as an adult. And though it may not be during this Thanksgiving, it is usually during the first years after high school that kids reveal to their parents that they are no longer Christians. Seventy-five percent (75%) of kids raised in Christian homes leave the faith when they leave home. If you have four kids, pick the three that you are willing to give up for eternity. When your child tells you that they are no longer a Christian, you have a different challenge on your hands. The 18 years you had with them is over. The years that they spent in Sunday school are gone. You will never again have that level of involvement and authority to speak into their lives.

Research tells us that most youth who leave Christianity are already mentally gone sometime in high school. What that means is that if you have a child in high school they have probably already closed their mind to Christianity, but are just waiting until they are out from underneath your roof before they say something. If you have a middle-schooler, they are headed that way too. Right when your newly independent, mature, intellectual child informs you that they are no longer a Christian is not the most strategic time to begin pleading with them and pulling out all the stops to save them.

Is it hopeless? No. However, on Monday when they drive back to school, they are under the influence of the world where you hold no credibility. Your influence over them will diminish as they become *smarter* and you hold onto your *illogical* faith. Getting those kids back to the faith is a much different issue and much harder task than the problem we are solving in this book. Prevention really is the best medicine.

The good news is that if they are still in your home, even if they have deep doubts, you have time. However, you must use that time dealing with the factors leading to their departure head on. The promise of this approach is that you will strengthen your child's faith in God and create a closer relationship with each other. The issue of salvation for your children is so important that it is not something to put off until tomorrow.

The challenge for us parents has always been how to give our children the best foundation for choosing Jesus Christ as their Savior so that we will eventually spend eternity with them. There is no exact answer for success because every person's path to a decision for Christ is different, and we each make that decision based on an incredible number of circumstances. Be encouraged because the part of the solution presented here is straight forward and very powerful. Before we discuss solutions in detail, you should understand the problem in greater depth.

Overview Research: Why Kids Leave the Church

Here is what we have learned from an extensive body of research conducted over the past 15 years. These are just a few of the results from some of the studies.

In 2002, the Southern Baptist Council on Family Life found that 88% of the children in evangelical homes leave church at the age of 18, never to return.[7] The research summarized in the book, *Soul Searching: The Religious and Spiritual Lives of American Teenagers*, found that the largest single reason students leave faith behind is because of intellectual doubt and skepticism.[8] Other sources are reporting

---

[7] The Southern Baptist Convention's Family Life Council
http://www.sbcannualmeeting.net/sbc02/newsroom/newspage.asp?ID=261

[8] Soul Searching: The Religious and Spiritual Lives of American Teenagers, by Christian

that, "63% don't believe Jesus is the Son of the one true God. 58% believe all faiths teach equally valid truths. 51% don't believe Jesus rose from the dead. 65% don't believe Satan is a real entity. 68% don't believe the Holy Spirit is a real entity."[9] Still others report that "no more than 15% of the total emerging adult population embrace a strong religious faith. They often have strong religious upbringing but tend to be more discriminating about what they will adopt."[10] "The majority of teenagers are <u>incredibly inarticulate</u> about their faith, religious beliefs and practices, and its place in their lives." The de facto dominant religion among contemporary U.S. teenagers is labeled, 'Moralistic Therapeutic Deism'. They believe that:

- A God exists who created and orders the world and watches over human life on earth.
- God wants people to be good, nice, and fair to each other, as taught in the Bible and by most world religions.
- The central goal of life is to be happy and to feel good about oneself.
- God does not need to be particularly involved in one's life except when God is needed to resolve a problem.
- Good people go to heaven when they die." [11]

Smith Pg 89 Published by Oxford University Press; Reprint edition (April 13, 2009)

[9] <u>Rethink: Is Student Ministry Working?</u> Steve Wright, InQuest Ministries, Inc. (2007)

[10] <u>Souls in Transition: The Religious and Spiritual Lives of Emerging Adults</u> (2009) by Christian Smith, Patricia Snell (2009)

[11] <u>Soul Searching: The Religious and Spiritual Lives of American Teenagers</u> by Christian Smith and Melinda Lundquist Denton, Oxford University Press, 2005

The Pew Research released in August 2016 shows that the exodus of kids from the faith and their explanations for why are ongoing and unchanging. Seventy eight percent (78%) say they were raised as a member of a particular religion before shedding their religious identity in adulthood. Some of the reasons given were "science," "I don't believe in miracles," "common sense," "logic," and a "lack of evidence."

From my own investigation of the reports and surveys, I have found that only 12.5% of high school graduates who were raised in Christian homes remain in the Christian Church. My numbers confirmed what the surveys are saying even though I calculated them using a completely different method. I started with the Pew Research Center numbers contained in their *America's Changing Religious Landscape* report released in May 2015 and incorporated U. S. population numbers, those turning 18 every year, and the known percentages of conversions to Christianity at different age groups. No matter how you measure it, the majority of kids raised in Christian homes are leaving the faith.

I like what George Barna said in his book *The Seven Faith Tribes*, "Suppress your urge to deny that what is said in these pages is true and significant. …When you hear the analysis of our situation, your task is not to like what has been presented, but to demonstrate responsible citizenship by strategically dealing with it."[12]

---

[12] The Seven Faith Tribes: Who They Are, What They Believe, and Why They Matter by George Barna, Tyndale Momentum Oct 1, 2011

Overview: Solving the Problem

It seems simple enough that the solution to our problem is to remove the reasons why kids leave the faith. The reasons kids leave are our targets. If a person rejects Christianity because they do not believe in miracles, then in order to remove that reason we must provide evidence in support of miracles. If a person leaves the faith because they do not believe that Jesus is the son of the one true God, then in order to remove that reason, we must provide evidence that Jesus is the son of the one true God.

In the Army we didn't get credit for firing our weapons, we got credit for hitting our targets. The research has provided us a consistent list of targets for addressing the loss of kids from the faith. Everything that we do in the education process that does not address or support the accomplishment of hitting these targets can be eliminated as wasted effort. Keep the worship time and keep the social time, but when it's time to teach, teach. We must learn how to expend our efforts in the most effective manner.

Current Methods: Are Not Working

We should be deeply discouraged that the majority of kids raised in Christian homes do not believe the central tenants of the Christian faith. Presumably, explaining how Jesus is the son of the one true God, that He rose from the dead, and that He is the only way to salvation have been the most frequently covered topics in our youth groups. Pastors, parents and Sunday-school teachers have covered these subjects in countless ways over a dozen years and yet;

- 63% don't believe Jesus is the Son of the one true God

- 58% believe all faiths teach equally valid truths
- 51% don't believe Jesus rose from the dead

Our current methods are not working. Can we in good conscience keep doing the same things in the same ways?

The list of reasons that the Pew Research Group gave us as to why young people leave the Church is what I believe underpins the lack of belief in the gospel. These are our targets.

A. They believe in science
B. They don't believe in miracles
C. They believe that there is no evidence

Can we in good conscience keep doing the same things in the same ways?

There is great reason for hope because when the cause of the disease is discovered, proper treatment can be applied. No one rejoices at an illness, but the stress of an illness is compounded when the causes are unknown. As soon as the cause is determined, we have hope because now we know that we can focus our attention on healing the disease.

We are going to heal the Church from the inside out. I'm proposing a proper diet and exercise not pills and surgery. I'm suggesting that we create healthy habits that maintain health, not short-term fixes that only present health on the outside. I believe that a modification of the habits of our youth education processes is necessary in order to heal the Church and begin revival.

Get excited and start eating your vegetables.

Solution: What and How

Our solution revolves around *what* we teach kids and *how* we teach them.

Church

Effective Teaching Methods, Answering Kids' Legitimate Doubts Using All Evidence in Order to Encourage Salvation

We are going to change *what* we teach our kids. We are going to teach them things that knock down their skepticisms. Can you write down three pieces of evidence to refute each of the areas of skepticism identified in the Pew research? If not, it's time to start studying. You are running out of time!

How: You Can't Tell Them

We are going to change *how* we teach our kids. <u>You must realize that TELLING these kids that Jesus is the Son of the one true God, that Jesus is the only way to salvation and that he rose again is NOT working for the majority of kids.</u> How many times have you and the Church already told them these things? The questions our kids are asking start with, "Why?" For example, "Why should I believe that the Bible is reliable?" and "Why should I believe that Jesus rose from dead?" If the thoughts you are having right now revolve around the impossibility of answering those questions, then take a breath and listen. The evidence for the reliability of Scriptures and Jesus' Resurrection is incredibly strong and multi-faceted.

What: Evidence

Evidence for our worldview is the *what* we need to teach our kids. When you take the time to look at the evidence, you will be satisfied beyond a reasonable doubt that Scripture is truth. Education is the beginning of enjoying your vegetables. Evidence cannot replace faith, but when you are satisfied that the Bible is true and that Jesus rose from the dead just as the Scriptures say, how much more confident are you in your faith? Now think about your kids. We can't tell them anymore, but we can teach them. Start lacing up your running shoes.

How: Testing and Measuring

Teaching our kids implies that they are learning, and currently we as a church do not measure what they are learning. The studies show that they are rejecting the core principles of our faith despite countless repetitions of the gospel. We must teach the Full Testimony of God, the gospel and the evidence that supports it, and we must measure the knowledge of our kids.

If we do not test them, then we cannot know if they have the intellectual foundation to understand that Christianity is the truth. We can't even know if they understand what it means to be saved.

As it is now we have no expectations from our kids. We spend 18 years with them hoping that they pick up Christianity through association rather than academics. We are socializing them, not teaching them. Sure, we do Bible studies and speak to them a lot, but what do they take away? No one can tell me because we don't measure it. We don't test them.

Why: No Defined Goals

When you look at the "What We Believe" sections on church websites, we see their core beliefs and the goals that they have for their different ministries including youth. We typically read that the church wants to prepare kids with a strong foundation in Christ. There is never any depth to what that really means. We don't see any deliverables. The goals of the church and each individual ministry should be spelled out in detail, by age and subject. For example, one of the specific goals might look like this;

> The Church will teach and test 11th grade students so that they are able to explain three sets of evidence that support the reliability of Scripture and it's authority in their lives.
> 1. Students will be able to describe how Scripture demonstrates characteristics as a document from a source that is outside of time.
> 2. Students will be able to describe the evidence for New Testament Scripture as eye-witness accounts written shortly after the life of Jesus.
> 3. Students will be able to understand why the New Testament is considered by scholars to be 99% accurate to the original manuscripts.

The power of such knowledge in the subject and in the entire list of doubts is what can help save our children and grow the Church. If pastors and youth pastors were guided to fulfill very specific deliverables such as these, we would remove many of the uncertainties and subjectivity of their current roles and evaluations. By having specific, measurable goals, Churches could identify those pastors who are unable to succeed in teaching and discipling our youth. The Church could evaluate individuals in responsible positions beyond the numbers of people in seats. Churches could clearly identify those that are providing an education that saves and those that are not. Like in business, it's not how much you make, it's how much you keep.

One challenge with implementing a clear system of expectations is that the people responsible for implementing the system are those that are currently enjoying very subjective standards of accountability. Instituting a set of clearly defined standards is a mission for the leadership of every church. Pastors, youth pastors, boards, deacons and parents should insist on having this as an agenda item at the next meeting. The benefits of clear expectations and accountability cannot be overstated.

Testing does not have to be exclusive to academic subjects. We can question and track our youth with regard to relationships, perceptions, challenges etc.. Questions on all kinds of subjects can give us a great deal of information that will give us a warning when a child is at risk of leaving the Christian Church.

I hope you are gaining a confidence in your ability to affect your children and the Church. You can.

My Testimony and the Logic of Apologetics

Perhaps this book is finding you at the place I was when I was first convicted to begin my study. I was having coffee with

Loren Ware, himself a father of three teenagers, when the subject turned to preparing our kids to defend their faith. My blood ran cold when we started discussing the questions with which the world would challenge our kids. Though we never attempted to answer the questions at that meeting, I was embarrassed because I knew of my inability to answer basic questions.

I engaged in the study of apologetics because I couldn't answer the questions that I knew the world was going to throw at my children. And if I couldn't answer those questions, then I knew my kids couldn't answer those questions. And if my kids could not answer those questions then they were at risk of leaving the faith. Chances are your kids don't know the following.

- They don't know why evil exists in this world and why a loving and merciful God could allow suffering.
- They don't understand that there is no evidence for the theory of evolution in spite of it being taught as a fact in school.
- They don't know that there is great evidence that the Bible is the accurate, eye-witness accounts of the events it describes, and that it hasn't changed since it was written.
- They don't know that the Universe, according to overwhelming scientific evidence had a beginning, and that a beginning demands a beginner, a Creator, a Cause.
- Your kids don't understand that it is possible to show beyond a reasonable doubt that Christ rose from the

grave and appeared to the disciples and over 500 other witnesses.

It's important to put apologetics in the proper context. When I started my journey to solve my lack of knowledge in these vulnerable areas, I didn't know what apologetics was. I had heard of apologetics, but had the same thought that many of you did when you first heard the word, "I don't have anything to apologize for."

The books I began to read did not have "Apologetics" in the title. They had titles like, *Tactics, On Guard, I Don't Have Enough Faith to be an Atheist,* and *Cold Case Christianity.* I read these books because they gave me the information I needed to achieve my goal, which was answering the tough questions of the world. I didn't read them to be an apologist, but in the process, I became an apologist.

What is an apologist? An apologist is someone that is capable of refuting the world's claims head on and providing evidence as to why Christianity is the truth. To me, that sounds very much like a disciple and a necessary skill for an evangelist. It seems to me that being an apologist is not a role reserved for the few silly people who can stay strapped in their seats long enough to understand the teaching, but it is required of everyone. 1 Peter 3:15 says, *"Always be prepared to give an answer to everyone who asks you to give the reason for the hope that you have."* If you are a Christian, then being a Christian apologist should be assumed.

If you are a Christian, then being a Christian apologist should be assumed

J. Warner Wallace of *Cold Case Christianity*[13] encourages everyone to become a $1 apologist. Mr. Wallace is contrasting the well-known apologists who write books, debate atheists and produce podcasts with the need for multitudes of people who can defend their faith in their daily lives. The educational process I am proposing is intended to mass produce $1 apologists.

Sadly, I was never encouraged by the church to become an apologist and though the area of study is the solution to many of the main problems in the Christian Church, it remains a marginalized pursuit. Through this book, you will understand the role of apologetics in helping keep your children and those in the Church Christian. You will also have a simple method for implementing powerful apologetics and Biblical teaching into your classrooms.

Church and Apologetics
You are preparing to learn how to defend your faith using evidence and logic. However, you need to understand that the area of study you are going into, Christian Apologetics, is not widely practiced by most churches. Your church will certainly know about apologetics and they can recommend some books and maybe even a member who likes apologetics, but for the most part, it is an afterthought. Apologetics have mostly been

---

[13] http://www.coldcasechristianity.com/

an individual pursuit and sometimes the subject of a bible study. Apologetics, in common Christian terms, is simply the defense of the faith. It is an area of study that is incredibly powerful in improving the chances that your child will gain a faith of their own. Apologetics is the substance of your diet and the bar bells for your exercise. It is not a cure-all, but it will help a lot.

The reason that churches shy away from apologetics is because it is predominantly academic and appeals to so few people. I may be one of three people at my church who would be thrilled to hear a sermon on the scientific evidence supporting the creation of the Universe. Everyone else would have to get up to go to the bathroom sometime during the lecture and wouldn't come back. The academic nature of the field of study makes it less appealing than reading and contemplating the Bible or listening to a sermon, but it is that aspect which also makes it so powerful.

My purpose is to solve the problem of the loss of kids from the Christian Church. When I chose my tools I didn't choose based on the easiest to carry or the most trendy, I picked them based on what works the best. The apologetics tool may be a bit heavier, but it works brilliantly – and it is fascinating.

Learning Apologetics to Save Our Kids
In the process of learning the evidence supporting the Christian claims, apologetics will take you through scientific and historic subjects and engage you in philosophical logic. You will begin to connect the dots between what you see in the world around you and the mighty power of our God. You will be able to walk your children along that same path, which leads to making a

real decision for Christ. The evidence reduces the gap between skepticism and faith. The bridge that they have to build from what they know to what is necessary for faith in the Christian worldview becomes shorter and shorter as they learn.

Right now our kids are going into high school and into the world without the answers to the questions that they need. Their intellect demands these answers, and they want their questions answered even though they don't ask you. There is no time like today to begin your incredible journey into learning about the evidence for the Christian faith. Though the area requires study, is your child's salvation worth overcoming any hesitancy about the work ahead?

There are a lot of practical objections to engaging in the suggestions I've presented. Where do the expertise and materials come from? What about theological intricacies that apologetics might confuse? How do I get the rest of the youth staff on board? We are already doing a great study and we have materials for the next year. I'm sure that I'm missing a bunch of reasons why now is not the right time to begin the process. However, if you agree with the premises and potential returns, I strongly suggest you begin to take steps toward implementing the solutions now.

Revival: The Payoff

The problems that we are solving are not tiny blemishes on the church body. The solutions are the actual muscle of the church body which strengthens every part. Our workouts will have an effect that changes the look and impact of the Church as a whole. We have the ability to produce revival in the country and around the world. Though we are focused on our own kids and congregations, we are part of the larger Church. By individually hitting the targets of skepticism, we can have a broad-based movement that advances the Church.

The Christian Church has been in defensive mode for far too long. We are losing our kids and we are losing members. Are you content that the Christian Church is only fading by .129% as a percentage of the U. S. population per year? I'm not. I believe that we can create revival in the Church. The most strategic segment of our Church that we can pour into is the youth. There are several reasons that identify our youth as the only real tinder for the fire of revival.

- Our youth are not yet lost. We can dramatically improve our trajectory as a Church if we simply keep the kids that we have. We as parents and as a Church are still able to speak into their lives. After the age of 18 that capability drops dramatically. Since they are not yet lost, they are not defending a worldview contrary to Christianity. Once they make the decision for anything besides Christianity, they will defend it to the death, which is a much harder battle for us to win. We are not losing adults, we are losing kids.
- Most Christians are saved by the age of 21. Sixty-four percent (64%) of Evangelical Christians are saved through High School and 13% from 18-21. Seventy-seven percent (77%) of adult evangelicals were saved by the age of 21. Older people are just as valuable in God's eyes, but from a strategic perspective, they require a lot of effort for low payoff. I can understand if it's distasteful to talk about people as statistics and

prioritizing one group over another, but our mission is not political correctness, it's saving our youth and our Church.

- Our youth are in the greatest natural evangelical environment of life's journey. Christian and non-Christian kids alike between the ages of 13-21 are searching for the proper worldview. Kids are together and meeting new people all the time. In most cases the worldview with the most educated spokesmen wins. We must educate our kids to educate other kids.

My proposition is that we begin to take back souls and win the souls that belong to God and allow a different eternity for millions of people.

Leadership

Leaders are by definition, leading. They are out front. They have an objective, they plan the most strategic path to achieve their objective, and then they move. The best leaders don't move without knowing where they are going and why. The educational solutions that I propose are intended to allow church leaders to implement the suggestions above with a full understanding of how to accomplish their goals. The solutions are fully compatible with current organizational structures, tools and leaders. They are within the grasp of laymen to lead effectively, and they teach and test. My purpose is to save souls and in the process we will fill youth groups, evangelize young adults and begin revival in the Church.

If the philosophy is implemented broadly enough the changes can be dramatic. In 40 years, if we are able to retain 40% of our high school students (vs. 25%), we will have an additional 20,441,177 Christians and giving of over $10 billion more than if the current trend continues. How much good in helping others can be done by the Church with additional resources? The revenue exceeds $47 billion if each person gives $2,315 per year. In 40 years, If we are able to retain 50% of our high school students and the 18-21 salvation increased from 13% to 23% and the post 21 percentage increased from 23% to 33%, then we will have an additional 48,709,826 Christians and giving of over $24 billion per year more than we would have if the current trend continues. Our revenue increases to $112 billion if each person gives $2,315 per year. The Evangelical Church would account for over 34% of the adult population as followers. That's a revival!

> **Please Return to the Beginning of the Chapter and Take the Post-Test**

Chapter 3: The Analysis

Take this Pre-Test prior to reading the chapter.

	Question	Pre-test		Post-test	
1	The loss of kids from the faith is a symptom of a larger problem.	T	F	T	F
2	The U.S. Government and Secular Society make it difficult for the Christian Church to thrive.	T	F	T	F
3	Millennials are fully capable of understanding and accepting Christianity.	T	F	T	F
4	Parents are turning over too much responsibility for teaching their kids to the Church.	T	F	T	F
5	The Gospel of Christ has lost its effectiveness in today's society.	T	F	T	F
6	The Church prepares the youth that stay in the faith to be evangelists.	T	F	T	F

7	The Bible has all of the answers that our kids need to face the world.	T	F	T	F
8	Testing youth in the knowledge that they gain each week is impossible.	T	F	T	F
9	Answering the critiques of the secular world is an effective way to strengthen Christian faith.	T	F	T	F

The Real Problem

The problem we are facing as a Church is that a massive amount of our youth are leaving the faith after high school. Our kids are so attracted to the secular world and they carry enough doubt in their hearts that they are able to leave the faith of their childhood and enter the world of ambivalence.

I have referred to the loss of kids from the Christian Church as the problem, but the fact is that it is only a symptom of the problem it's not the problem itself. Furthermore, the loss of Christian kids is only one of the symptoms. The other symptom is that 66% of Americans are casual Christians. Only 17% of Americans would be considered Captive Christians, "Those whose consistently Biblical beliefs and Christ-like behavior validate their commitment to being followers of Christ."[14] Other symptoms include:

---

[14] Ibid

58

- The shallow faith of our youth that stay
- Their low level of biblical literacy
- Their misunderstanding of the core tenants of Christianity
- Their low competency in evangelizing

The loss of kids from the Christian Church is only a symptom of the problem

I will use a manufacturing process as the model to better illuminate the situation and the causes of our problems. Manufacturing is rather impersonal, but as a model it allows us to isolate different factors that may or may not be impacting our final product, the faith of our kids. So though the terms are impersonal, we can never lose sight of the fact that each statistic, each *product* is one of our children. Each of our children has a life that will be lived in joy with a relationship with Christ and an eternity in Heaven, or the opposite. The important part of this model is that it helps clarify the causes of our problems so that we can begin work in the proper areas to correct our processes.

The Machine

Think of a machine. We pour raw material into the top and turn the machine on. It begins to churn away. It makes a loud chugging noise and smoke begins to come out of the top. Sparks fly every which way until finally it spits out a finished product. We pour infants into the top of our Church machine.

We expend huge amounts of time, energy and effort into forming Bible-believing, Spirit-lead products. 18 years later we open the church doors and present our products.

The things that happen inside of our machine determine what kind of product it is. Seventy five percent (75%) of our products fail quality control testing. They walk out of the doors and a fire-breathing dragon immediately gobbles them up. We wanted a Christian. What we produced was a skeptic. A high portion of those that remain are passable, but the paint melts easily in the dragon's fire to show the shoddy workmanship. Only a small percent venture on to be Captive Christians – those Christians with a fire-proof shield, helmet and a sword.

What Are We Trying to Produce?

Though it's pretty clear that we are not producing what we want, we need to define what it is we are actually trying to achieve. For what purpose are we really producing our product? What is our product supposed to accomplish? In the previous chapter I introduced the fact that we need to start teaching apologetics and testing their knowledge. If we left our solution at that, you could accomplish much. We would begin to keep many more youth in the faith. However, in this chapter we are going to start drilling down into what the Bible wants us to produce and the inertia that we need to overcome in order to do so. Simply put, we are supposed to be producing Scripture-following Christians who live out their faith and fulfill the Great Commission.

> *(Romans 10:9) [9] If you declare with your mouth, "Jesus is Lord," and believe in your heart that God raised him from the dead, you will be saved. (John 3: 16) [16] For God so loved the world that he gave his one and only Son, that whoever believes in him shall not perish but have eternal life. (Ephesians 2:8-10) [8] For it is by grace you have been saved, through faith—and this is not from yourselves, it is the gift of God— [9] not by works, so that no one can boast. [10] For we are God's handiwork, created in Christ Jesus to do good works, which God prepared in advance for us to do. (Romans 12:2) [2] Do not conform to the pattern of this world, but be transformed by the renewing of your mind. Then you will be able to test and approve what God's will is—his good, pleasing and perfect will. (1 John 2:3-4) [3] We know that we have come to know him if we keep his commands. [4] Whoever says, "I know him," but does not do what he commands is a liar, and the truth is not in that person. (Matthew 28:19-20) [19] Therefore go and make disciples of all nations, baptizing them in the name of the Father and of the Son and of the Holy Spirit, [20] and teaching them to obey*

everything I have commanded you. (1 Peter
3:15) Always be prepared to give an answer to
everyone who asks you to give the reason for
the hope that you have.

We are on solid Biblical ground to expect that our goal as
parents and as a Church is to produce adults who are Captive
Christians. The Church and parents are responsible for the fact
that we are not doing so. Let's face it, there is no one else
trying to accomplish this mission so the responsibility has to
rest on us. The irony is that I have witnessed the extraordinary
efforts that my churches and other parents have expended to
produce the best product. I will assume the same of most
congregations.

We all fervently care about the salvation of our kids. There
is no lack of quality Biblical material, one-on-one
communication and relationship building. There are an untold
number of programs and events in which our kids can
participate. The churches in which I have been involved are
determined, regardless of the discomfort, to address social
issues directly. They discuss the proper Christian attitude
towards homosexuality, pornography, and promiscuity. They
deal with the heart issues of love, forgiveness and generosity.
We seem to be closely following the Biblical recipe, so why is
our product so poor?

Possible Causes for the Failure of Our Products
Let's examine the highlights of things that might be responsible
for our failure to produce a large percentage of quality

products. Why are 75% of kids raised in Christian homes leaving the faith after high school?

1. Is the <u>Government too restrictive</u> of Christian rights?
2. Are <u>youth not smart enough</u> to grasp key Biblical concepts?
3. Are <u>youth not motivated enough</u> to study God's word?
4. Have <u>parents turned over too much</u> responsibility to the church?
5. Are <u>youth pastors ill-prepared</u> to teach the gospel to youth?
6. Are <u>churches not putting enough emphasis</u> on youth groups?
7. Has the <u>Church not worked hard enough</u> to prepare our youth for the world?
8. Are Churches not teaching the <u>right subjects</u>?
9. Are Churches using <u>poor processes</u> to prepare youth?
10. Has the <u>Gospel of Christ lost its effectiveness</u>?
11. Has <u>science produced so much evidence</u> that Christianity is no longer intellectually sustainable?
12. Is the <u>public education</u> system too secular to combat?
13. Is the <u>self-focused message of culture</u> too pervasive and too powerful to fight?

This is just a partial list of the possible causes, but I believe it is a good representation of all of the categories. Except for #10, there is probably some truth to each of these possibilities. To varying degrees each of these causes affects our ability to create the products we want. And though #10, the Gospel of

Christ, has not lost its effectiveness, we have clearly failed to penetrate our kids' hearts with it. I will expand on each of these possible causes in the following pages.

1. Possible Cause: US Government

If you look at the list, notice that I put it in rough manufacturing order. The U. S. Government impacts every manufacturing process in the country. They mandate many health and safety practices, material qualities and labeling.

The Government, despite legislating from an increasingly secular value system, has not directly impacted the ability of the Christian Church to operate freely within its doors. Churches can produce its youth using any reasonable method they deem fit. Pastors are allowed to say what they please and members are free to come and go as they wish. If the Church has sermons every day of the week expressing its views on abortion, homosexuality and divorce, then grab a program and have a seat. The government won't stop it. The government is not the problem.

2. Possible Cause: Youth

The next set of possible causes of our problem have to do with the raw materials. Could it be possible that our youth are simply substandard material from which to produce Captive Christians? It's a valid question considering the ubiquitous criticism of the millennial generation, but I'd suggest that the material is just fine. Certainly millennials have different perspectives based on the era into which they were born, but they are just as fully capable as any generation before them. They have the ability to grasp concepts and learn in the same way that we did in the 1970s, 80s and 90s before the internet and texting. And like us, they probably have very little motivation to study – anything – including the Bible. Though we would like them to study the Word of God, I believe that we can impact them in spite of their lack of study. The lessons that we can provide them in the hour a week that we have them will give them a solid enough foundation to reasonably decide to remain a Christian. Our youth are not the problem.

3. Possible Cause: Parents

To be blunt, parents are the primary cause of the loss of youth from the Church. That's not to say that many parents are not deeply concerned with the salvation of their kids. They desperately want to spend eternity with their children, but they are quite often at a loss as to how to pass on their faith. Nevertheless, Scripture places the responsibility for the godly upbringing of children on the parents, not the Church and not the *village*. Deuteronomy 6:5-9 says:

> *5 Love the Lord your God with all your heart and with all your soul and with all your strength. 6 These commandments that I give you today are to be on your hearts. 7 Impress them on your children. Talk about them when you sit at home and when you walk along the*

road, when you lie down and when you get up.
⁸ Tie them as symbols on your hands and bind
them on your foreheads. ⁹ Write them on the
doorframes of your houses and on your gates.

And again, Proverbs 22:6 says, "Start children off on the way they should go, and even when they are old they will not turn from it."

Unfortunately, the majority of parents do not hold their own Christian faith as a high priority and they don't demonstrate faith in their daily lives. It is tough enough for those of us earnestly seeking God, but studies tell us that most

parents are not even trying. These are parents who do not love God with all of their hearts and don't act as if they do. This creates a two-fold problem where on one side the parent is not that concerned about their child's faith development and on the other side they demonstrate a hypocritical example for their kids.

When the church teaches the kids *to forgive others as God has forgiven them* and then they see their parents fussing about the other drivers on the way home or hear them complaining about the pastor's lack of attention to them after the service, they get the picture. Parents' actions during the time that the family is not in church are more revealing to kids than how they act during the hours spent among the congregation.

Martin Luther's thoughts on the subject as paraphrased by Fredrick Nohl were that "too many parents fail to teach their children because the parents don't want to be bothered, don't know how, or don't have the time."[15] This condition is as true today as when Martin Luther expressed it in 1524.

For all of our picking at the millennial personality, one thing that they rightly demand is authenticity. When their parents set an inauthentic example as Christians, the kids notice. The main reason our machine (the Church) is getting material that is resistant to its message is because of parents. Parents can coat an otherwise fine material with a thin layer of oil which makes the teaching of the Church slide right off.

As we watch the young generations leave the faith, we are reminded of what quickly happened to the young Israelites when their parents didn't follow God's commands. In only a generation after God collapsed the walls of Jericho and two since He parted the Red Sea, the Israelites fell away.

> *(Judges 2:10-11) [10] After that whole generation had been gathered to their ancestors, another generation grew up who knew neither the Lord nor what he had done for Israel. [11] Then the Israelites did evil in the eyes of the Lord and served the Baals.*

The encouraging news is that if you are a parent desiring to influence your kids to stay in the faith, you have a great chance of doing so. As a parent who loves the Lord you should take the responsibility for becoming someone capable of teaching and guiding your children properly. The suggested solutions in

---

[15] Luther: Biography of a Reformer Hardcover by Frederick Nohl, Concordia Publishing House September 1, 2003

this book will help you immensely. Do not accept any excuse for being ill-prepared to teach your kids the gospel or to teach them how to defend the Scriptures from the attacks of this world.

God not only gave parents the responsibility, but also gave them the ability to accomplish the mission. Parents' influence is a determining factor in the directing their kids. Kids follow their parents. A National Study of Youth and Religion quoted by David Briggs reveled that;

> *"Just 1% of teens age 15 to 17 raised by parents who attached little importance to religion were highly religious in their mid to late twenties. In contrast, 82% of children raised by parents who talked about faith at home, attached great importance to their beliefs, and were active in their congregations were religiously active as young adults, according to data from the latest wave of the National Study of Youth and Religion.[16] The connection is 'nearly deterministic,' said Christian Smith, lead researcher for the study and a sociologist at the University of Notre Dame in Indiana."[17]*

We can acknowledge that raising Christian kids is not easy, but it is no excuse for not doing everything you can. Any parent who has tried to lock down their computers and electronic devices from pornography can tell you it's a horrifying, confusing, never-ending job. Trying to teach our

---

[16] http://www.thearda.com/Archive/Files/Descriptions/NSYRW3.asp

[17] Parents are top influence in teens remaining active in religion as young adults by David Briggs November 5, 2014 https://www.christiancentury.org/article/2014-11/parents-no-1-influence-teens-remaining-religiously-active-young-adults

kids to live biblically in a pornographic, hostile world is even more difficult. Parents facing the reality of this challenge cannot count on the Church to do the heavy lifting when it comes to setting a daily, godly example and teaching our faith.

Though parents are the root of the problem, I do not believe that parents as a group are the practical source of the solution. By that I mean that the majority of parents will remain in blissful ignorance of the problem and unwilling to put in the effort to help their kids. I, therefore, have focused on solving the problem through the organization of the Church. You, as a determined follower of Christ moved to impact youth can volunteer at your Church to help change the course of your children and others.

I cannot end this section without encouraging you to pray for your kids, their friends and their future. Pray in the name of Jesus concerning the challenges that they are facing now and those that you know are coming. Plead for protection from the enemy and for wisdom in fighting the spiritual battle that rages all around.

4. Possible Cause: Church

Though the parents are part of the supply chain, for our purposes, the Church is the machine. The Church has a structure, paid leaders, set times to meet and instruct, curriculums, and organized youth groups. Churches are the place where the raw materials are worked on for 18 years. Without relieving parents of any of their responsibilities, if we are to be transparent, let's also acknowledge that most parents will not or cannot fulfill their responsibilities. This is not right and not as it should be, but it is an unfortunate reality. The

Church is where we will corporately make or break the next generation of Christian youth. By saying next generation, what I really mean is that you can start to affect every student, including the high-school seniors this coming Sunday. This does not have to be a slow process of revival.

The Christian-making machine we call the Church may be responsible for the faulty products in multiple ways. Certainly, the Church is not solely responsible, but I believe that it is the Church that must pick up the mantle, claim responsibility, and do its best to fix the problem. If not the Church, then who?

5. Possible Cause: Church; Youth Pastors and Youth Groups

There is no doubt that most youth pastors are prepared to teach the gospel and that there is plenty of emphasis on youth groups. Churches are working their tails off to prepare our youth for the world, but for the  most part they are failing. This brings us to the next two subjects which are the most responsible for the difficulty that Churches are having keeping kids in the faith.

6. Possible Cause: Church; Subjects and Processes

Since we are choosing to set the responsibility for fixing the problem at the Church's feet, then there are only two possible causes of the problem that remain within its control. I believe that Churches are not teaching the right subjects and they are using poor educational processes to prepare youth. When I discuss the right subjects, it means that they have a proper mix and focus on the right subjects. There is no suggestion that teaching the gospel and biblical perspectives is wrong, but is it enough? I have already introduced the main concepts of the *What* (Full Testimony of God) and *How* (measuring/testing) of teaching as the solutions to our problem. In this section we will examine some root causes to our problem that revolve around subject matter and process. This analysis will take us to a deeper understanding of the inner workings of our machine and which components need adjusted.

7. Possible Cause: Church; Fatigue and Testing

No matter what subjects we teach, we will have to deal with normal challenges of student attention and interest. Bringing our youth up in the Church is much like applying paint to our product. We apply layer after layer of beautiful

Christian-theology paint onto the plain surface of our youth groups every week. We do big roller strokes on the younger ones and carefully applied edging to the older kids ready for more precise knowledge. As they grow, we admire the rich colors that are developing and we attempt to cover some of the thinner areas with more coats of paint. It is a lot of work conducted by countless teachers and lead by Pastors following the latest philosophies of becoming relevant to the new generation. Then after 18 years of painting, we send the kids into the world. Unfortunately, when we look at our youth-group kids within one year of graduating high school, 75% of the paint has peeled off. The product is a mostly bare, splotchy, peeling mess. Only a few small areas have the deep color we applied, while the few other places where color still exists, are faded or discolored. What in the world is happening?

The surface of our product is completely unprepared for the application of paint. There is no primer. The resistance to theological paint starts young. This is easy to test. How much do you pay attention to the road or directions when you are the passenger in a car? We tend to zone out or pay attention to other things when we aren't responsible for getting our passengers to the destination. We are especially prone to wandering thoughts when we believe we know where we are going.

The next time you are teaching Sunday school or just talking to your middle-school kids, ask them if they know the story of Adam and Eve. What about telling a high-schooler that you are going to cover the story of Noah's Ark? The sighs and rolling of the eyes will tell you all that you need to know. These kids have heard these stories a thousand times before. They think that they know where you are going, and so they tune out. Eyes wide open, heads nodding, tuned out.

As you are uncovering deeper lessons in the well-worn Bible stories, the kids are in the passenger seat not paying attention. You discuss the nuance of Satan's deception of Eve and how that relates to how Satan tempts each of us, and your students are still hearing the story they heard in elementary school: Adam – Eve – Apple – Sin – Bad. This is the first step in a damaging set of circumstances that is keeping our kids from fully embracing the Word of God. You discuss the faith of David or Abraham and the kids picture Goliath and a burning bush. They are not picking up on the deeper theological points or life-application importance of the examples.

Don't get me wrong, we as painters are doing our best to paint the product. We are clever in how we use music and video and practical exercises to engage kids, but because they believe that they already know it all, most of it drips to the floor.

Eyes wide open, heads nodding, tuned out

The lessons we give to kids as they get older are perfectly reasonable lessons with additional verses, facts and nuances appropriate for their increasing maturity. However, because they have already tuned out they are not getting the lessons. Then, as we layer different social guidelines on top of a child-level theology, kids have a hard time understanding. They are not reconciling their childish understanding of Adam and Eve and sin, and God's judgment, and Jesus' sacrifice with why they should think one way or another about homosexuality, pornography and monogamy. It is very sad to say, and I have tested this multiple times with older kids, there is even a lack of understanding of what it means to be a Christian.

Kids do not know the basic standard for being a Christian. They do not understand, and they cannot summarize the key points of Christ's sacrifice, what it means, or how we should respond to it. This premise is also easy to test. With your own kids or on Sunday morning when you speak to your youth group have each kid write down the answer to the question, "How do you become a Christian?" We joke about getting the church answer to our questions while in church, but you will be surprised at how many kids really answer, "Believe in God."

We spend all of our time painting, and we stand back to discover that the center of the product, the very area that should be the best covered, has peeled just as badly as the rest. Though we've tried, we are failing to secure the hearts and minds of our kids.

This gap in the knowledge of the foundation of Christian theology starts at the youngest ages. As the kids grow older, they presume they have heard it all. Then they begin to engage their intellect and their critical-thinking skills. Unfortunately, that aspect of their God-given being is not addressed in youth groups consistently. We don't give them answers to their questions about the reliability of Scripture, why evil exists, the reasonability of Jesus' rising from the dead, and a worldwide flood. The world is challenging them with tons of other questions that revolve around the truth of Christianity, and as we have seen, it is a major reason why kids are leaving the faith. This compounding of the problem means that they don't understand theology and their intellect starts to tell them that it is not true anyway, so they don't need to learn it. They are left without a foundation of both the heart and the head.

We are teaching the right subjects, but we are not teaching enough subjects. We are not addressing the reasons why they should believe Christianity to be true. As processes go, we are not testing and measuring their knowledge and so

we have no idea that they have been passengers zoning out through the past several years. Covering biblical subjects with apologetic subjects in a coordinated way reduces the know-it-all syndrome because we get to ask really interesting questions that mean something to them in authentic ways.

For instance, "What would happen if the force of gravity were slightly different?" Did you know that if the force of gravity were different by one part in 10^{60} (10 with 60 zeros behind it) life wouldn't exist? Science tells us that God put extraordinarily precise forces into our universe from the instant of creation in order to sustain the life He gave us. Walk through this lesson and many other lessons with your kids and God can become very real to them. They've heard that God created everything, but now they can see the pencil marks on His blueprint and how He did it all for a purpose.

Beyond expanding the subjects taught in order to maintain the attention of kids and satisfy their intellectual curiosity, testing and measuring of their knowledge is critical. Expect them to learn it. We are putting out a lot of energy to teach them. They should be expected to learn the material. I am not suggesting that we create our own standardized testing that qualifies them to be a Christian, but we should have much higher standards than we currently have.

Here's the scope of what I'm talking about. Like the Bible stories our kids hear over and again, you have heard the public service announcements about the dangers of smoking more times than you can count. What if, instead of only seeing and hearing advertisements about smoking, the government put you into a class where you had to learn the mechanism by which smoke chokes off the oxygen to living cells and kills them?

Then the instructors taught you the different medical conditions that come about as a result of prolonged smoking, and they take you to visit emphysema patients in the hospital. You would have to learn vocabulary, key facts and graphics. You would see the evidence for yourself. You would have to observe an autopsy of the lungs of a smoker and a non-smoker to see the difference. Throughout your course of instruction the teachers would give you tests to take to review your knowledge.

If you were to engage in that level of instruction, would you have a much deeper understanding of the dangers of smoking? Would you be able to discuss the decision to smoke much more intelligently than if you were simply parroting an advertisement? That's what I'm suggesting for teaching Christianity. Teaching a proper mix of subjects combined with proper testing and measuring, is a layer of primer on our product that allows the paint to stick. Without that primer, we are trying to apply paint to an unprepared surface and that will rarely work.

As valuable as teaching the evidence for Christianity is, and how illuminating the testing process will be, there are other adjustments to our machine that must be made. I said that our goal is to produce Christians capable of carrying out the Great Commission. It is not an easy task, and it demands that our kids can defend themselves against the secular worldview as well as evangelize.

8.   Possible Cause: Church; The Great Commission

The Purpose setting on our machine needs to be turned way up. I believe that our modern Christian teaching of what it means to fulfill the Great Commission shies away from demanding the hard work that Jesus expects.

I read the Bible and get convicted of the evangelizing I'm supposed to do. Then when I hear a sermon on evangelizing and the harder obligations of engaging with the world are ignored or rationalized away, I secretly take comfort. I'm perfectly comfortable believing that by living a life that reflects God's work in my heart that I've done enough. But I know that it's not enough.

We talk about living a life that is different enough from the world that it encourages people to ask what makes us different.

We want to be so godly that people are attracted to the fruit in our lives. We envision long-time acquaintances taking us to lunch and asking, "Why are you always so joyful?" Then, we get to lovingly present our testimony and invite them to Church. We want to think that living as an example is active evangelism.

Living a Godly example is an essential part of the Christian's mission, but it is not active evangelism. The importance of that aspect of our daily walk cannot be emphasized enough, however, is there more that Jesus is calling us to do? As I have been examining the characteristics of what we want to produce through our youth programs, the Scriptures draw me to the example that Jesus and the disciples set in building the early Church.

In Scripture we see their work clearly before us and it is read from the pulpits week after week, and yet I can't remember consistently being challenged to engage the world in a way similar to how they engaged the world.

Living a Godly example is an essential part of the Christian's mission, but it is not active evangelism

---

In breaking down the actions of Jesus and the disciples I'm not suggesting that modern Christians do things exactly as they did. Let's face it; they acted out an amazing faith that is convicting for anyone attempting to mimic their lives.

However, we can look at the characteristics of *how* they evangelized to gain insight into what is expected of us. We can determine if we are creating products capable of engaging with the world at a level similar to that of the disciples.

Are we even trying?

We know that the disciples were proselytizing in the synagogues. Let me emphasize right away that I'm not suggesting modern Christians walk to the front of a Synagogue or Mosque or Temple and begin to argue for Christ. Though we don't need to prepare to walk into other places of worship and confront different congregations, I will argue that our machine is not set anywhere near where it needs to be in order to produce people that impact the world in the way the disciples did.

The disciples and the apostles were engaging with the world from within Jewish Synagogues. They walked right into the place of worship of the people to whom their message was blasphemy, and boldly proclaimed the truth. At the risk to their lives, health and freedom, they walked straight up to the podium and began to present the case for Jesus as the Messiah. More than that, they argued using the evidence from the Jewish Scripture. This would be like a Republican walking into a Democratic fundraiser and confidently and effectively making an argument for the Republican candidate as President. They didn't do this just once and then quickly run out, they did it over and over again – for years. And why did they consider this level of confrontation necessary? Perhaps it's because they were following the example of Jesus.

(Matthew 9:35) Jesus went through all the towns and villages, teaching in their synagogues, proclaiming the good news of the kingdom and healing every disease and sickness.

(Luke 4:42-44) [42] They tried to keep him from leaving them. [43] But he said, "I must proclaim the good news of the kingdom of God to the other towns also, because that is why I was sent." [44] And he kept on preaching in the synagogues of Judea.

(Matthew 13:54-55) [54] Coming to his hometown, he began teaching the people in their synagogue, and they were amazed. "Where did this man get this wisdom and these miraculous powers?" they asked.

(John 18:20) [20] "I have spoken openly to the world," Jesus replied. "I always taught in synagogues or at the temple, where all the Jews come together. I said nothing in secret."

Jesus' teaching in synagogues and the Temple is not disguised in the Bible, and it is a clear example of how we should engage the world. At least that is what the disciples and apostles believed. The reason Jesus warned them about the dangers to come is because they would be expected to put themselves in danger.

> *(Mark 13:9-10)* [9] *"You must be on your guard. You will be handed over to the local councils and flogged in the synagogues. On account of me you will stand before governors and kings as witnesses to them.* [10] *And the gospel must first be preached to all nations.*

> *(Luke 12:11-12)* [11] *"When you are brought before synagogues, rulers and authorities, do not worry about how you will defend yourselves or what you will say,* [12] *for the Holy Spirit will teach you at that time what you should say."*

And Jesus gave them the Great Commission.

> *(Matthew 28:18-20)* [18] *Then Jesus came to them and said, "All authority in heaven and on earth has been given to me.* [19] *Therefore go and make disciples of all nations, baptizing them in the name of the Father and of the Son and of the Holy Spirit,* [20] *and teaching them to obey everything I have commanded you.*

After Jesus' ascension we see the disciples and apostles follow his command. Certainly the early church had outdoor teaching and the home church, but it was in the synagogues that the Church met the world in direct competition.

> *(Acts 6:9-10) [9] Opposition arose, however, from members of the Synagogue of the Freedmen (as it was called)—Jews of Cyrene and Alexandria as well as the provinces of Cilicia and Asia—who began to argue with Stephen. [10] But they could not stand up against the wisdom the Spirit gave him as he spoke.*

It was in the Synagogues where the Church found its contention, credibility and early converts.

> *(Acts 9:20-21) [20] At once he (Paul) began to preach in the synagogues that Jesus is the Son of God. [21] All those who heard him were astonished and asked, "Isn't he the man who raised havoc in Jerusalem among those who call on this name?"*

> *(Acts 13:5) [5] When they arrived at Salamis, they proclaimed the word of God in the Jewish synagogues.*

> *(Acts 14:1-3) [1] At Iconium Paul and Barnabas went as usual into the Jewish synagogue. There they spoke so effectively that a great number of Jews and Greeks believed. [2] But the*

*Jews who refused to believe stirred up the
other Gentiles and poisoned their minds
against the brothers.*

And watch what happened next. When the Jews who refused to believe stirred up trouble, Paul and Barnabas didn't run away. Instead, Scripture says that it was *because* of the converts and the dissention that they stayed. In the next verse it says, *³ So Paul and Barnabas spent considerable time there, speaking boldly for the Lord, who confirmed the message of his grace by enabling them to perform signs and wonders.*

The fact that our common understanding of Christian responsibilities of evangelism does not highlight this aspect of the Great Commission demands that we spend a little bit more time with it. The example of the disciples and the apostles is so over-the-top clear, that it must be emphasized so that we have an undeniable standard by which to grade our products

*(Acts 18:7-9) ⁷ Then Paul left the synagogue
and went next door to the house of Titius
Justus, a worshiper of God. ⁸ Crispus, the
synagogue leader, and his entire household
believed in the Lord; and many of the
Corinthians who heard Paul believed and were
baptized. ⁹ One night the Lord spoke to Paul in
a vision: "Do not be afraid; keep on speaking,
do not be silent.*

God spoke to Paul because Paul was afraid. He might not have shown it on the outside, but he was afraid, otherwise God's words would not be necessary. Paul's habit was to go into the synagogue and reason with the Jewish worshipers. And though he did it consistently, it does not mean that he was always fearless on the inside. God reinforces everything that Paul was doing. He was consistently in the synagogues, he was speaking to the people, and God says, "Do not be silent."

> *(Acts 5:40-42)* [40] *They called the apostles in and had them flogged. Then they ordered them not to speak in the name of Jesus, and let them go.* [41] *The apostles left the Sanhedrin, rejoicing because they had been counted worthy of suffering disgrace for the Name.* [42] *Day after day, in the temple courts and from house to house, they never stopped teaching and proclaiming the good news that Jesus is the Messiah.*

Is there any question that the disciples and apostles believed that Jesus called them to engage the world in the most confrontational set of circumstances possible? Has this calling been eliminated or are we still called to engage the world that way? What reason could Jesus possibly have to put the men and women he loved into harm's way? Jesus tells us that his purpose is to save the world.

> *(John 3:16-17)* *For God so loved the world*
> *that he gave his one and only Son, that*
> *whoever believes in him shall not perish but*
> *have eternal life. For God did not send his*
> *Son into the world to condemn the world, but*
> *to save the world through him.*

In order to save the world, Jesus told them to

> *(Matthew 28:19) "Go and make disciples of*
> *all nations, baptizing them in the name of the*
> *Father and of the Son and of the Holy Spirit."*

If you are stuck on the idea of going into synagogues to confront Jewish worshipers with the evidence for Christ, relax, because I don't believe that Jesus is calling modern Christians to do that. Though early Christians preached at risk to their life, I don't believe that they did it in environments that were so quarrelsome that no message could be shared. They were able to get their message out, argue about it, and then be killed.

You may not pay with your life today, but it is much harder to get your argument clearly heard. In many cases, you don't need to get any farther than the name of Jesus before you are shut down. Walking into a mosque to preach would not be a prudent move. However, we are still commanded to get our message to the world and into those places of discomfort, in front of groups who disagree with us, and where our personal safety may be at risk.

Let's make this personal and go through an exercise we should be able to do with our kids when they are properly prepared for the world. Take a moment to think about the groups or people to whom you would most fear talking. Would you be more apprehensive about making the case for Christianity to a group of Jews, Muslims, Mormons, Atheists, Scientists or New Agers? Would you rather get a seat on a plane next to a chatty college student studying Zen Buddhism or an evolutionary biologist?

Now let's put it a different way. If God was to give you an assignment to go to one type of non-Christian to minister, to which would you most prefer to go? For which group or type of people is your heart the softest? The disciples had a heart for their own people. They deeply desired to bring the good news to their fellow Jews. For whom do you have a heart?

It may be helpful to consider the characteristics of the synagogue for the early believers.

1. The disciples loved their fellow Jews. The disciples went to them. The synagogue is where they gathered. Who do you love and where do they gather?

2. The Jewish Scriptures held much of the evidence that pointed to Jesus as the Messiah. The disciples were able to use the information that they were jointly familiar with to argue for Jesus'. The disciples had to be prepared to support their faith with evidence. What are the beliefs of the group you want to go to and how can you use that information to reinforce the evidence for Christ? Science, for instance, has provided ample evidence for the existence of a designer of the Universe

and life. Can you support the Christian faith with scientific evidence?

3. The synagogues offered a forum for the disciples' message to be heard even though it challenged Jewish beliefs. The disciples found a place where they could be heard out. Where is that for your group? Are you educated and practiced enough to engage with that group?

4. There was immediate argument, counter points, anger and emotion from the Jews. The disciples had to be prepared to defend their faith. How prepared are you to defend the Christian faith?

5. The disciples put their freedom, well-being and lives in danger every time they preached in a synagogue. Is the love you have for others worth the risks you will have to take – the risks to which Jesus is calling us?

Jesus said to go make disciples of all nations and he clearly set the example and expected his followers to go into the synagogues. What does he also expect from us?

This level of commitment demands that we love others enough to overcome our fear of rejection and humiliation. It demands that we educate ourselves on our own beliefs and those of our audiences. We must practice and prepare to engage with others who believe differently, and we must be courageous. When we as a Church sidestep the demands of scripture to actively go into the world (neighborhood) and make disciples, we also eliminate any urgency to be educated, prepared and courageous. I am not dismissing the internal challenges of self-control that we all go through to live lives honoring to God; however, those challenges are only a part of the mission to which God has called us.

When we as a Church sidestep the demands of scripture to actively go into the world (neighborhood) and make disciples, we also eliminate any urgency to be educated, prepared and courageous

---

As we examine the capabilities of the kids we are sending into the world, we realize that we had the "Purpose" setting of the machine way too low and that we added too much water in the process. By evading the difficult teachings of Scripture we actually lowered the standard of what was necessary to be an effective Christian. We watered it down. If there is no demand to be educated, prepared and courageous, all of which are uncomfortable, then those goals will not be  accomplished. Youth don't completely know why Christianity is unfulfilling to them, but it is. The Christianity that the machine teaches does not require any work. The religion really has no purpose beyond living a good life, which they believe that they can do without the rules.

One of the prime missions of the Church is to present God's true demands on Christians, and youth in particular. When we set as a goal the production of kids who can fulfill the Great Commission, the deeper purposes of the added apologetics subjects and of the testing become clear. We as a Church will begin to realign our work with our stated priorities. We will become authentic with regards to the alternative worldviews and the impact that they are having on our youth.

Neil T. Anderson from his book, *Victory Over the Darkness* puts it this way,

> *"Those distortions often arise when the church is not living up to its potential. Consequently, many people think the church is an infirmary where sick people go. We limp along in unbelief, hoping the rapture will come soon and take us out of this miserable defeat. The church is not an infirmary; it is a military outpost under orders to storm the gates of hell. Every believer is on active duty, called to take part in fulfilling the Great Commission."*[18]

The core of the Great Commission is that we as a Church are engaging the culture in the arena of ideas. We are expected to face all contrary ideas and beliefs and have the ability to overcome their arguments and point people to the truth. That

---

[18] Victory Over The Darkness, Realize the Power of Your Identity in Christ, by Neil T. Anderson, Bethany House 2013. Page 114

has always been the situation. It's not that our generation is any more corrupt or godless as we might like to think, it's that we have become less practiced in the work and processes necessary for competing effectively. Without expecting this level of evangelism from our church and without preparing our kids properly, there is no capacity for revival.

We have identified two of the major settings that we must adjust on our machine, <u>Attention</u> and <u>Purpose</u>, and how they relate to our methods and expanded subjects of teaching. It is a good time to reemphasize that the gospel has not lost its effectiveness in the Church, but it has lost power in the society. By arming our kids with only the gospel, we put them at risk of buying into the other ideas in the arena. They never really stand a chance of overcoming the competing ideas and beliefs because we have never told our side of the story. If we look at making a case for our faith only from a defensive perspective, then we are missing the fact that we are called to be on the offensive. We are called to win souls, not simply maintain as much of what we already have as we can.

9. Possible Cause: Public Education, Self-Focused Society and Scientific Evidence

Our last three potential causes for the loss of kids from the faith revolve around the environmental conditions in which our products are produced and in which they are expected to function. Our kids are raised in and grow into adulthood in our society. During the production process our church machine is presenting a message counter to the public education system, the self-focused message of popular culture, and against the

secular scientific foundation, which underlies both education and moral attitudes.

This section is important to explore because our products, our kids, are supposed to work effectively as evangelists in this society and yet we sometimes complain that the system is too tough to fight. We must immediately remove that type of thinking from our minds.

Blaming the broken society that we are supposed to fix for our inability to fix it is a poor excuse. Helplessness like that is akin to using a feather duster to turn a bolt and blaming the bolt for our lack of progress. We are sending feather dusters into the world instead of wrenches...or power-wrenches. If our job is to produce Scripture-following Christians who live out their faith

and fulfill the Great Commission, then by definition, they must do that in our society. Right now our machinery is calibrated to produce feather dusters, and therefore we produce feather dusters. We have disregarded the job they are supposed to do in spite of the signs telling us we need to produce wrenches.

Blaming the broken society that we are supposed to fix for our inability to fix it is a poor excuse

By adjusting the settings in our machine to teach an expanded set of subjects using effective educational methods, we will begin to produce wrenches. Our products will actually work in the world.

Products in Society

The signs are telling us to educate our kids against the attacks of the world. The studies have revealed why youth are leaving the faith and given us the targets that we identified in the previous chapter.

    A. They believe in science

    B. They don't believe in miracles

    C. They believe that there is no evidence

    D. They don't believe Jesus is the Son of the one true God

    E. They believe all faiths teach equally valid truths

    F. They don't believe Jesus rose from the dead

By enacting an educational system that overcomes these skepticisms, we will produce products that are capable of fulfilling their purpose in the world. The public education system and society promote naturalistic causes for supernatural events like the creation of the Universe and the creation of life. Their conclusions are supposedly backed by scientific evidence. However, these conclusions cannot withstand the truth. Here's the truth; science, history and philosophy at the highest levels point to a designer and a savior. We have time to train our youth to use the evidence *of the world* to refute the *skepticisms of the world.* Our youth can walk into the synagogue of science, open the book and argue for the existence of God using their *scriptures.* They can walk into the halls of history and philosophy and prevail in those discussions. And, they can do it with love, understanding and compassion.

Somewhere along the manufacturing line, as we teach the Full Testimony of God, apologetics alongside the gospel, the self-focused message of culture will lose its irresistible power.

When our youth accept Scripture as truth intellectually, spiritually and experientially, it becomes real in their life. The words that God gave us for living our life to the fullest mean something when the Bible means something to the person  reading it. The goal of my suggestions is not intellectual, it's spiritual. My goal is to produce spirit-filled youth who become confident, Christ-following adults. It is through salvation and the Holy Spirit that we know and are reconciled with God. The gospel is the meat and potatoes. The intellectual aspects of apologetics is the plate on which they sit. The cold, hard plate of apologetics supports the warm, tasty, nourishing gospel.

The gospel is the meat and potatoes. The intellectual aspects of apologetics is the plate on which they sit

Organize your manufacturing plant to teach apologetics with the Biblical message together. Apologetics can be considered the complimentary message from God, and together with the Bible, the complete testimony of God. God gave us the evidence that supports his Word. Let's use it.

10. Possible Cause: The Gospel of Christ has Lost its Effectiveness

I cannot leave this section of the analysis without covering in greater depth the possible cause that the Gospel of Christ has lost its effectiveness. This analysis considers that 25% of youth that remain Christians after graduating high school with the current teaching methods and subjects of the Church. Without minimizing that number I'd suggest that they are more feather duster than wrench. Our youth are primarily armed with a message that the world does not understand and which is not optimal for competing in the arena of ideas.

The Bible: Single Point of Failure

We must produce products that are able to compete in the arena of ideas and win. The ultimate idea of Christianity is salvation through Christ. Our kids are competing in the world with a Biblical concept that puts them at a disadvantage. Not only do we know from the studies that our kids are theologically illiterate, even when they do engage the world they are speaking a language foreign to the world. If all they understand is a biblical perspective, with biblical justifications and language, in the best case, they will be prepared to function in the confines of Christian cloisters. Our youth may thrive in the world, but only by separating their Christian identity from their public, professional identity.

Our kids are unable to translate Christianese into Secularese. A person passionately professing the gospel in Russian to an English audience will have no effect at all. Since they live in the secular world, they learn to communicate about secular subjects in secular ways. Faith is not supported in this language from secular sources and so the kids are unable to effectively defend their faith or evangelize. Our youth stumble to find the foundation of their faith in the Bible in light of the 'new' evidence of the secular world.

The Bible is a single point of failure that our kids don't know how to defend. "The Bible tells me so," is a single point of failure that is costing Christianity dearly. Why?

Not, "Why is it costing us dearly," but, "Why is Scripture to be believed as truth?" That is the question that the world is asking our youth. This is a "Why" question that we must prepare our kids to answer.

We all agree that Scripture is the infallible word of God, but it is wrong to send graduating high schoolers into the world with that as their only answer to the world's attacks.[19] This

---

[19] Paul writes, in 2 Timothy 3:14-17, "[14]But as for you, continue in what you have learned and have become convinced of, because you know those from whom you learned it, [15]and how from infancy you have known the Holy Scriptures, which are able to make you wise for salvation through faith in Christ Jesus. [16]All Scripture is God-

simple question, "Why is Scripture to be believed as truth?" takes 95% (maybe more) of Christians out of their depth and yet it is the first question the world inherently asks our kids. Why can't you drink to excess? Why can't you have promiscuous sex? Why can't you get revenge or be angry or unforgiving? Why can't you seek your own pleasure? Why is not wealth the greatest measure of a person's value? There are secular answers to these questions such as disease, illness and lack of fulfillment, but the only Christian answer is because the Bible tells me so.

At the vulnerable ages of 14-19, when youth are beginning to think critically, take notice of the opposite sex, and assert their independence, many are hoping that the Bible is not true. If the Bible is not truth, then none of these things are prohibited. This age group is exceptionally vulnerable to deception because in their minds they would be ok if the Bible wasn't true. If the Bible is only true because my pastor and parents say so, then I think I'm going to err towards the evidence and follow my friends and my hormones. Pastor Andy Stanley contends,

> *"Unfortunately for you, when you went off to college or you went into adulthood, you ran into information that made the Bible from your perspective indefensible, and it was a house of cards. And all somebody had to do was show you a part of it was questionable and the whole thing came tumbling down and most of you*

breathed and is useful for teaching, rebuking, correcting and training in righteousness, [17]so that the servant of God may be thoroughly equipped for every good work."

were glad it did because you didn't really want
to be a Christian anyway. And now you had an
intellectual reason to walk away from the faith
that was hampering you." [20]

The Church was given a belief system with a single point of failure – Scripture, but we were also given multiple sets of evidences that overwhelmingly support its reliability. This is the relationship of Scripture as the meat and potatoes and apologetics as the plate on which it sits. Unfortunately, most of our kids leave 18 years of Church education with one defense, "The Bible tells me so."

Kids have never had instruction in or been tested on the internal evidences of fulfilled prophecy or external evidences of third-party validation. They don't know when the books of the Bible were written or how they were passed to us today. They don't know anything about the documentation of the Old Testament, the Dead Sea Scrolls or what they mean to verifying the truthfulness of the New Testament. They can't tell you what is broadly accepted as the historical facts of Jesus' life or how the lives of the disciples and the beginning of the Church logically support Jesus' resurrection.

We must be strategic in our preparation of the next generation of Spiritual Warriors. We know where the enemy is going to be. He's been there since the Garden of Eden. He will attack the Word of God through deception and by tempting us with the fulfillment of our sinful desires. If we know that Satan

---

[20] Who Needs God? The Bible Told Me So a sermon by Pastor Andy Stanley Aug 27, 2016 http://northpoint.org/messages/who-needs-god/the-bible-told-me-so/

is sitting there waiting for our kids then why are we allowing them to walk past him without arming them in every way possible?

Adam and Eve failed despite knowing God. Their inherent curiosity and pride was sufficient material for Satan to get them to destroy their own lives. Our kids face the exact same challenge, but with one great advantage, we know the attack is coming and we can warn and prepare them. If we are only teaching them the Bible and not the evidence and arguments that support the truth of the Bible, then we haven't fully prepared them.

God told Adam and Eve not to eat from the tree. They knew the Word of God – straight from His mouth! Likewise, our kids have heard the Word of God too many times to count, but what is it that will get them to choose the Word of God over their personal desires at the point of temptation?

If we know that Satan is sitting there waiting for our kids then why are we allowing them to walk past him without arming them in every way possible?

Our churches must be deliberate in instructing our children in the evidences for the reliability of Christian Scripture. Imagine our kids at the point of temptation wrestling in their mind with whether or not they should step off the path. There is not anything physical holding them back – another drink, another touch, another peek. Is the Scripture real to them? If it is, then they won't be thinking through the arguments for the eye-witness accounts or the 99% accuracy of the text or fulfilled prophecy, their heads will be where they should be, knowing God is real, that He is watching and protecting them in this battle. That's what will make a difference when it really matters.

Lita Cosner and Scott Gillis at Creation Ministries International support the evidential approach.

> *"The Bible tells me so" faith will likely not sustain people when they encounter objections to the faith. But the answer is not to so easily dismiss the authority and inerrancy of Scripture, but rather learn how the evidence supports the historical account of the Bible."* [21]

God set up a single point of failure; and success – Jesus Christ. And Jesus Christ is only believable if Scripture is believable, and Scripture is only believable to people if the critiques of this world are refuted by evidence. If that single point is not supported by every possible defensive and offensive strategy, then it will often fail. The failure to instill reasonable belief in the Bible is why we are seeing 75% of our youth leave the Church for good after high school and the remaining 25% join a passive evangelical Christian culture.

---

[21] Pastor Andy Stanley says the Bible is too Hard to Defend by Lita Cosner and Scott Gillis, 22 September 2016 http://creation.com/andy-stanley-rebuttal

Possible Causes Summary

We have examined the possible causes responsible for our failure to produce a large percentage of quality products and why 75% of kids raised in Christian homes leave the faith after high school. In summary, we are not restricted by our government. Our youth are smart enough and as motivated as any generation before them. Parents have turned too much responsibility over to the Church, but not more than the Church can handle. Youth pastors are prepared. Churches are working hard and are putting plenty of emphasis on youth groups. Scientific evidence is on our side. We are not victims of the public education system or of the self-focused message of culture. Unfortunately, Churches are not teaching the full-range of necessary subjects and are using poor processes to prepare youth.

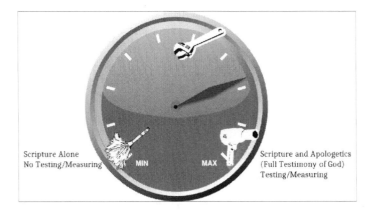

Scripture Alone
No Testing/Measuring

MIN   MAX

Scripture and Apologetics
(Full Testimony of God)
Testing/Measuring

In order to produce God-loving, Great-Commission fulfilling products, you and your church must start teaching and testing the Full-Testimony of God. When you do, the symptom of the loss of kids from the Church will be dramatically reduced and the foundation for revival will be set in place.

Please Return to the Beginning of the Chapter and Take the Post-Test

Chapter 4: The Solution

Take this Pre-Test prior to reading the chapter.

	Question	Pre-test		Post-test	
1	Any new curriculum that cannot be effectively conducted by lay teachers will fail.	T	F	T	F
2	Any new curriculum that requires substantial changes to church structures and schedules will not be accepted.	T	F	T	F
3	Any new curriculum that does not measure results will fail to produce the desired results.	T	F	T	F
4	Having students read a page of material during class would take too much time.	T	F	T	F
5	Answering a set of questions about the reading is an effective way of engaging students' intellect.	T	F	T	F

6	Discussing apologetics subjects is not possible for the vast majority of volunteer teachers.	T	F	T	F
7	It is unlikely that youth will tolerate taking tests of 20 questions or more every week.	T	F	T	F
8	Youth know that Scripture is the infallible Word of God.	T	F	T	F

The implementation of an educational system that properly teaches the Full Testimony of God is not as difficult as people might suspect. Achieving the goals that we have set through this book is easily within reach for any church or parent. However, it is necessary to create materials that allow for lay teachers to teach the subjects with little preparation and which can be covered in less than an hour. At this stage, we are describing the characteristics of acceptable solutions to our problem. We've spent a great deal of time identifying the things that we need and the things that we want to avoid. This phase of planning is very much like describing the characteristics of your next vehicle.

If you have a farm and it's just you and your spouse, you might want to get a two-seat pickup truck. If you have five kids and lots of activities, a mini-van would be more appropriate. The characteristics of the vehicle are based on your needs. If you choose a truck to haul a large family around or a mini-van to haul hay, you could rightly be accused of poor planning. The kind of vehicle the Church is looking for is one that will carry 100% of the students, not just 25%.

Let's walk through the design of our solution that will make it effective in accomplishing our goals. I have a step by step guide to this process in the next chapter.

The solution conforms to several critical criteria;
1. Subject Matter
2. Accessibility
3. Compatibility
4. Measurability
5. Duration

1. Subject Matter: The Process Must Teach the Proper Subject Matter

The content of classes must contain a substantial amount of material that presents evidence in support of the Christian worldview and refutes the claims of other worldviews. Apologetics, as explained throughout this book, is the area of study that directly addresses the reasons that kids are leaving the faith.

2. Accessibility: The Process Must be Accessible.

The subject material must be formatted in a way that allows for use by lay people with very little preparation. That means that churches provide teachers with a packet of information, in the same way they are given lessons today, and with a little bit of reading and review they can confidently lead a class of students.

Accessibility can be accomplished in several ways. Youth pastors, parents or staff can easily create a weekly lesson or entire curriculum for free based on the information that is available to them in books they already have on their shelf or from the internet. They can also download materials from my website specifically designed for these purposes.

3.   Compatibility: The Process Must be Compatible.

The process must be capable of conforming to existing church structures. The materials must be able to work when teaching individuals, small and large groups. The materials must be able to fill different amounts of time that groups use for their instruction. The content must be theologically consistent with the beliefs of the individual group or church. The material must stand alone week to week in order to include new students and those who sporadically attend class.

Compatibility is inherent in the design of the lessons suggested here. Each lesson is customized by the person leading the class for time and content. Every lesson can be used with any size group. The church does not need to change the length of classes or gather additional resources that would not otherwise be needed. Teachers can use the most rudimentary tools like pen and paper or the most high-tech gear they wish. Each lesson is a complete lesson on its own.

4.   Measurability: The Process Must Measure

Measuring is the partner component to apologetics and is important whether teaching apologetics or the gospel. If the process is not testing or measuring the kids' knowledge in some way, it is not going to be effective.

5. Duration: The Process Must Allow for Various Class Durations

The process must be able to be effectively taught in the hour per week that the Church has the kids for class.

I've developed lessons formatted according to the standards below which are available for download and I encourage others to create and post lessons for others to utilize. The instructions for creating and teaching on subjects and with theologies that are specific to your congregations are available to you.

The Format of the Lessons

Proper formatting of the weekly subjects is critical to accomplishing something in our time with our students. Our goal is to educate them and know that they have been educated. We are going to accomplish this by formatting our lessons into five parts.

1. Cumulative test
2. Pre-Reading test
3. Reading
4. Discussion
5. Post-Reading test

Reading

I'm going to start with the Reading part since everything else derives from it. The reading section involves the students reading an article or chapter that covers the subject that you want them to learn. During class the students silently read the material. Depending on your time requirements it can be a paragraph or a page or more. There are tons of wonderful biblical and apologetics materials available. One technique could be to pull down a one-page article from the internet and use it as your reading.

In preparation, the youth pastor or teacher reads the material and identifies the three to five key points that they want their students to take away from the lesson.

Pre-Reading Test

Using those key points as the focus of the class, the teacher will prepare a pre-reading test. The questions should be written in a way that takes advantage of the student's misconceptions or ignorance of the subject matter. These questions don't have to be tricky, but the purpose is to set the stage for letting the students realize that they actually learned something in their time in class on Sunday morning. It is always more powerful for a person to see for themselves that they learned something rather than for someone else to tell them. The technique also automatically makes the teacher an authority.

I typically phrase questions with True/False, Yes/No answers. On rare occasions I'll give a multiple choice or fill-in-the-blank for the pre-reading test. The questions can be presented using a projected slide or on hard-copy handouts. It is important to be able to track each student's progress throughout the weeks so that they and others can see how much they've learned. I'll get to some examples at the end of this section.

The students take the pre-reading test before doing the reading. The student is then required to read the material. Reading during class is important for a few reasons. Reading includes all of the students in the class, it requires actual effort on the part of the student and it makes the pre-reading test effective.

The attendance in Sunday school classes varies from week to week, so handing out the material prior to class for the students to read may not include all of the students, and you would have to hand it out again during class anyway. Not to be cynical, but handing out materials ahead of time is usually ineffective because students will not even remember it until they pick up their Bible to come to class the next Sunday, at which point they will read it quickly and then answer the pre-test questions or show up to class without it and say that they forgot.

By requiring actual effort from our students it aids in the learning and retention of the material. This is the first time that students will see this material, but not the last.

Discussion

After the reading, the teacher engages the class in discussion, questions and answers, and teaching. The lay teacher can ask a series of questions about the reading. The teacher can repeat the focus points and teach from the article. The pastor preparing the lesson can list some suggested discussion questions, or allow the teachers in their preparation to do so. It is simple enough at the least to cover the pre-reading questions during the discussion. The pastor preparing the lesson is free to use as many discussion questions as necessary to help this process.

Post-Reading Test

The students will then do their Post-reading test. The post-reading test is the exact same test as the pre-reading test. Presumably, they will get all of the questions right this time and realize how much they learned in such a short time.

If the lesson does not last the entire class length, the teacher can move on to a common Biblical subject, interact with the kids on a more relational topic, or any number of subjects or activities.

Cumulative Test

The Cumulative test is a growing set of questions taken from the previous weeks' reading tests. Week one will not have a cumulative test. The questions on the cumulative test cover the same subjects, but can be more detailed than questions on the pre/post-reading tests simply because the kids have gained more detailed knowledge of the subject.

For example, on week two, the focus areas from week one will be put into a test and given at the very beginning of the class. In the week one pre/post-reading tests the question might be, "Does the Old Testament contain prophecies that are fulfilled in the New Testament?" That, of course is a Yes/No question. In the reading, you may have covered that Jesus' life, death and resurrection fulfilled over 300 Old Testament prophecies. On the cumulative test you could ask the more detailed question, "Jesus' life, death and resurrection fulfilled over _____ Old Testament prophecies."

You can see how we covered fulfilled Old Testament prophecies in a more specific manner in the cumulative test. Of course, if you wish to keep the questions the same as they go from the pre/post-test to the cumulative test, that is fine too.

You should prepare a limited number of easily answered questions per lesson. There is no homework or hard studying to do in order to answer the cumulative test questions each week, but the growing test is extremely powerful. In week two there may be five questions to answer, but in week three that number grows to 10; five from week one and five from week two. The questions from week one, week two etc. are exactly the same on the cumulative test as it grows in the number of questions each week. Answering the questions becomes routine and mundane after a few weeks and the kids go through the test quickly. My son answered the 16 questions on the week-four cumulative test in about 45 seconds.

After 10 weeks, the test has approximately 45 key biblical and apologetics questions that the kids can answer. This may sound like a lot, but it takes only a few minutes as the kids see the same questions over and over again.

How much of a difference would this make in the engagement and power of your youth? Certainly, much depends on the subjects that you are teaching. If a student has five pieces of evidence for the reliability of scripture that they can quote without much thought, how much of an impact will that make in their perspective on the meaningfulness of the Bible in their lives?

Will lessons on forgiveness, and service and sacrifice have more impact on them because they know for certain that the Bible is the Word of God? Will they accept that the teaching on homosexuality and promiscuity are God inspired and protective and not made up by man to be intolerant? Will they be ready when someone challenges their belief in the Bible?

The purpose of the educational process is to transform lives. Lives are transformed when the God's word becomes real to the person. Whether you are supporting the Creation story through scientific evidence or showing that Jesus' resurrection is the only reasonable conclusion from the evidence, the teaching and measuring you do is to guide these young people to their own decision for salvation.

As simple as the teaching process is, it is a dramatic departure from the direction the Church has been going. The process promises to:

1. Directly address the causes of the problem of the exodus of kids from the Christian faith
2. Solidify the faith of youth so that they seek to glorify God through their lives
3. Prepare kids to fulfill the Great Commission

The subject matter and teaching process presented here can address nearly the entire set of intellectual justifications for leaving the Church. Science, logic, miracles and evidence are precisely what apologetics covers. Rejecting apologetics as a major component of the solution is purposely choosing to travel uphill to the west in spite of the signs pointing you in the other direction. But speaking about apologetics along with scripture is not enough, we must actually teach and test our youth's knowledge of the information we are presenting.

I believe that when the intellectual barriers are removed the gospel can make a deep spiritual impact on our youth. I propose that our first objective is the establishment of Scripture as reliable in the minds of our youth. EVERYTHING follows from that knowledge and belief. Once Scripture is real, the lessons and messages of Scripture have value to the reader.

Please Return to the Beginning of the Chapter and Take the Post-Test

Download multiple *TESTED is Trained* formatted teaching series at the Resource section of www.BraceBarber.com. Each lesson comes with a short video preparation guide.

Join us for insights, discussion and community at https://www.facebook.com/bracebarberauthor/

Step by Step

This is a Step by step example of how to develop a solid lesson for the coming week. We are going to format our subject into five parts.

1. Cumulative test
2. Pre-Reading test
3. Reading
4. Discussion
5. Post-Reading test

Reading

Every portion of this format is derived from the Reading section. The first thing we want to do is select our reading material for the week. The sources of this material are endless. You can do anything from taking a page from a book you are reading to a passage from the Bible, to searching the internet for a good article that covers the subject you want to teach. For an hour long class you should only need one page worth of reading.

For our example, we are going to use an article written by J. Warner Wallace from Cold Case Christianity. I used this article in the third week of teaching about the reliability of Scripture. The evidence on which I focused revolved around the lives and commitments of the authors of Scripture. For the purposes of this example, I left the article exactly the same as you can find online. Normally, I edit out some parts to make for a clearer focus on the points I want to highlight.

I went to www.coldcasechristianity.com and searched for "Reliability of Scripture," and poked around until I found what I was looking for.

I chose this one:

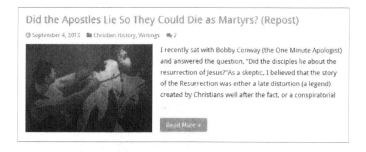

The sources and searches are endless. Look at a Google search for "Reliability of Scripture."

What if you are doing a class on the question, "Why is there evil?" Here are the results form a Google search.

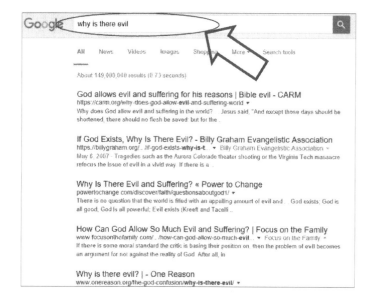

When preparing the lesson, you may have to read through a few articles before you actually find the perfect article to support your purpose. After finding the one you want, read through and highlight the points that you want to make.

Here are the points I highlighted in the article I chose. The numbers and highlights are mine. Read through the entire article for yourself so you understand the subject. You'll see how the reading connects to the focus points and the tests.

Did the Apostles Lie So They Could Die as Martyrs? (Repost)

http://coldcasechristianity.com/2013/did-the-apostles-lie-so-they-could-die-as-martyrs-repost/

By J. Warner Wallace

Cold Case Christianity

I recently sat with Bobby Conway (the One Minute Apologist) and answered the question, "Did the disciples lie about the resurrection of Jesus? "As a skeptic, I

---

believed that the story of the Resurrection was either a late distortion (a legend) created by Christians well after the fact, or a conspiratorial lie on the part of the original Apostles. It wasn't until I started working homicides (and homicidal conspiracies in particular) that I decided an Apostolic conspiracy was unreasonable. I've written a chapter in *Cold Case Christianity* describing the five necessary elements of successful conspiracies, and none of these elements were present for the Apostles. But even more importantly, the Apostles lacked the proper motivation to lie about the Resurrection. My case work as a homicide detective taught me something important: there are only three motives behind any murder (or any crime, or sin, for that matter). ①All crimes are motivated by financial greed, sexual lust (relational desire) or the pursuit of power. If the Apostles committed the crime of fraud on an unsuspecting world, they were motivated by one of these three intentions. Most people will agree that none of the Apostles gained anything financially or sexually from their testimony, but some skeptics have argued the Apostles may have been motivated by the pursuit of power. Didn't these men become leaders in the Church on the basis of their claims? Couldn't this pursuit of leadership status have motivated them to lie? Wasn't it a goal of early martyrs to die for their faith anyway?

The Apostles Knew the Difference Between Ministry and Martyrdom

The Book of Acts and the letters of Paul provide us with a glimpse into the lives of the Apostles. The Apostles were clearly pursued and mistreated, and the New Testament narratives and letters describe their repeated efforts to avoid capture. The Apostles continually evaded capture in an effort to continue their personal ministries as eyewitnesses. The New Testament accounts describe men who were bold enough to maintain their ministry, but clever enough to avoid apprehension for as long as possible.

The Apostles Knew the Difference Between a Consequence and a Goal

These early eyewitnesses were fully aware of the fact that their testimony would put them in jeopardy, but they understood this to be the consequence of their role as eyewitnesses rather than the goal. That's why they attempted to avoid death as long as possible. While it may be true that later generations of believers wanted to emulate the Apostles through an act of martyrdom, this was not the case for the Apostles themselves.

The Apostles Knew the Difference Between Fame and Infamy

It's one thing to be famous, but another to be famously despised. Some of us have attained widespread fame based on something noble (like Mother Teresa). Some of us have attained widespread fame because of something sinister (like Adolf Hitler). ②The apostles were roundly despised by their Jewish culture as a consequence of their leadership within the fledgling Christian community. If they were lying about their testimony to gain the respect and admiration of the culture they were trying to convert, they were taking the wrong approach. The Apostles only succeeded in gaining the infamy that eventually cost them their lives. This was obvious to them from the onset; they knew their testimony would leave them powerless to stop their own brutal martyrdom.

As I examine the motives and consequences related to the testimony of the Apostles, I still find their martyrdom to be one of the most powerful evidences related to the veracity of their testimony. Think about it for a minute: twelve designated eyewitnesses travelled the known world to testify to the Resurrection. ③Not a single one of them recanted their testimony. ④Not a single one of them lived longer because of their testimony. ⑤Not a single one benefitted financially or relationally. These folks were either crazy or committed, certifiably nuts or certain about their observations. As Easter approaches, it's time to take the testimony of the Apostles serious

Pre-Reading Test

I picked out five things on which I wanted to focus, and from these I developed four questions for the pre-reading test. As you know already, the pre-reading test and post-reading test are one in the same. Here are the questions that I came up with.

	Question	Pre-test		Post-test	
1	The Apostles gained an enormous amount of wealth as the heads of the Church.	T	F	T	F
2	The Apostles lived longer than the average person because of the better healthcare they could afford.	T	F	T	F
3	Some of the disciples took back their story about Jesus and his resurrection.	T	F	T	F
4	The Apostles were despised in the Jewish community.	T	F	T	F

You can see that all of these questions are extremely easy to answer once you've read the article. However, your students may have never thought about these facts or they may be misguided in how they thought about the subject. Are you beginning to see the power in this approach? After this class, when one of our kids is told by the world that Scriptures are corrupt because of greedy disciples, or because they wanted the easy life, they know better.

In the next figure, you can see how I formatted the questions at the top of the page that I use in class. Each student gets a copy or you can use some sort of projector or monitor and let the kids answer the questions on a separate sheet of paper. I hand out hard copies and fold each page over at the dotted line so that each student can only see the questions. This way they can take the pre-test without looking at the article.

8th Grade Men 9:30   Reading #3   Name:_____   Date:_____
Are The Scriptures Reliable?

	Question	Pre-test		Post-test	
1	The Apostles gained an enormous amount of wealth as the heads of the Church	T	F	T	F
2	The Apostles lived longer than the average person because of the better healthcare they could afford	T	F	T	F
3	Some of the disciples took back their story about Jesus and his resurrection	T	F	T	F
4	The Apostles were despised in the Jewish community	T	F	T	F

Did the Apostles Lie So They Could Die as Martyrs? (Repost)
http://coldcasechristianity.com/2013/did-the-apostles-lie-so-they-could-die-as-martyrs-repost/
By J. Warner Wallace
Cold Case Christianity

Dotted line

I recently sat with Bobby Conway (the One Minute Apologist) and answered the question, "Did the disciples lie about the resurrection of Jesus? "As a skeptic, I believed that the story of the Resurrection was either a late distortion (a legend) created by Christians well after the fact, or a conspiratorial lie on the part of the original Apostles. It wasn't until I started working homicides (and homicide conspiracies in particular) that I decided an Apostolic conspiracy was unreasonable. I've written a chapter in *Cold Case Christianity* describing the five necessary elements of successful conspiracies, and none of these elements were present for the Apostles. But even more importantly, the Apostles lacked the proper motivation to lie about the Resurrection. My case work as a homicide detective taught me something important: there are only three motives behind any murder (or any crime, or sin, for that matter). All crimes are motivated by financial greed, sexual lust (relational desire) or the pursuit of power. If the Apostles committed the crime of fraud on an unsuspecting world, they were motivated by one of these three intentions. Most people will agree that none of the Apostles gained anything financially from their testimony, but some skeptics have argued the Apostles may have been motivated by the pursuit of power. Didn't these men become leaders in the Church on the basis of their claims? Couldn't this pursuit of leadership status have motivated them to lie? Wasn't it a goal of early martyrs to die for their faith anyway?

The Apostles Knew the Difference Between Ministry and Martyrdom
The Book of Acts and the letters of Paul provide us with a glimpse into the lives of the Apostles. The Apostles were clearly pursued and mistreated, and the New Testament narratives and letters describe their repeated efforts to avoid capture. The Apostles continually evaded capture in an effort to continue their personal ministries as eyewitnesses. The New Testament accounts describe men who were bold enough to maintain their ministry, but clever enough to avoid apprehension for as long as possible.

The Apostles Knew the Difference Between a Consequence and a Goal
These early eyewitnesses were fully aware of the fact that their testimony would put them in jeopardy, but they understood this to be the consequence of their role as eyewitnesses rather than the goal. That's why they attempted to avoid death as long as possible. While it may be true that later generations of believers wanted to emulate the Apostles through an act of martyrdom, this was not the case for the Apostles themselves.

The Apostles Knew the Difference Between Fame and Infamy
It's one thing to be famous, but another to be famously despised. Some of us have attained widespread fame based on something noble (like Mother Teresa). Some of us have attained widespread fame because of something sinister (like Adolf Hitler). The apostles were roundly despised by their Jewish culture as a consequence of their leadership within the fledgling Christian community. If they were lying about their testimony to gain the respect and admiration of the culture they were trying to convert, they were taking the wrong approach. The Apostles only succeeded in gaining the infamy that eventually cost them their lives. This was obvious to them from the onset; they knew their testimony would leave them powerless to stop their own brutal martyrdom.

As I examine the motives and consequences related to the testimony of the Apostles, I still find their martyrdom to be one of the most powerful evidences related to the veracity of their testimony. Think about it for a minute: twelve designated eyewitnesses travelled the known world to testify to the Resurrection. Not a single one of them recanted their testimony. Not a single one of them lived longer because of their testimony. Not a single one benefitted financially or relationally. These folks were either crazy or committed, certifiably nuts or certain about their observations. As Easter approaches, it's time to take the testimony of the Apostles seriously.

Discussion

After the students read the article, the class has the opportunity to discuss the information facilitated by the teacher. It is my opinion that asking questions that force the kids to come to conclusions for themselves is the most powerful technique. We as a church have been telling kids what to believe since they were young. We now have the ability to ask questions such as, "Would you die for something that you knew was a lie?" "Do you believe anyone would die for something that they knew was a lie?" "If the apostles didn't gain wealth, power or relational benefits from building the church, why did they take the risk?"

Post-Reading Test
Once the discussion time is over, have the students retake the reading test and answer the questions in the post-test column. They should see that in the short time you had with them they actually learned something.

Cumulative Test
Let's extend our process out a bit farther and really strengthen our kids' faith and courage. By creating a Cumulative test we are reinforcing the lessons of previous weeks. The purpose of this test is not to fool the kids or test deep knowledge of the subject matter. The purpose of the test is repetition. We are asking the same questions week after week after week. Every week we are adding the questions from the previous week so that it grows in length but not difficulty. The questions can be more specific in the Cumulative Test, but should be easily remembered as main facts from the reading or discussion. The example about Old Testament Prophecy is a good one. We went from a broad question on the pre/post-test to a specific one on the Cumulative Test.

Cumulative Tests are given before the reading each week. Below is the Cumulative Test that I will give my students at the beginning of week number four. At this point we have done three weeks of reading and have 14 questions that are easy for the students. As the weeks go on I will mix up the order of the older questions just to keep them on their toes, but I will not change the questions unless the answer has been clearly covered in class. After students have taken the test, it is perfectly reasonable to walk through some of the questions and answers to reinforce the ones you believe may be confusing or troublesome.

Barber 8th Grade Men 9:30   Test #3

Name:_____ Date:_____

1.	About how many Old Testament Prophecies were fulfilled by Jesus? _____		
2.	If a book contains fulfilled prophecy's that have hundreds of years between the prediction and the fulfillment of the prediction what do we know about the source of that information?		
3.	Did the Old Testament predict that Jesus would be born in Bethlehem?	Y	N
4.	Are there prophecies in the Bible that have not come true yet?	Y	N
5.	The Old Testament predicted that Jesus would be buried with the rich.	T	F
6.	In whose tomb was Jesus buried?		

7.	The New Testament was written by the	T	F

	disciples over the course of several months in Jerusalem.	
8.	The New Testament has been purposely altered many times by those copying the Bible throughout the centuries	T F
9.	The Bible is how accurate compared to the original writings	41% 57% 99%
10.	We have thousands of ancient copies of the New Testament	T F

11.	The Apostles gained an enormous amount of wealth as the heads of the Church	T F
12.	The Apostles lived longer than the average person because of the better healthcare they could afford	T F
13.	Some of the disciples took back their story about Jesus and his resurrection	T F
14.	The Apostles were despised in the Jewish community	T F

In a standard 14-week bible-study curriculum your students will be quickly answering 60-70 questions. Sixty to 70 questions designed with the purpose of arming our kids for battle with the world.

It would be fair to say that the technique is elementary. It is absolutely basic. However, it would be wrong to say that it is not remarkable. Since we are talking strategy we can't miss the opportunity to quote Sun Tzu from *The Art of War*, "All men can see these tactics whereby I conquer, but what none can see is the strategy out of which victory is evolved."

Church

Effective teaching methods, answering kids' legitimate doubts using all evidence in order to encourage salvation

This approach is shockingly effective when you realize that through a simple technique we can satisfy every last demand necessary to reduce the exodus of Christian kids from the faith.

- This method can be explained in a matter of minutes and produced from scratch by a layperson in less than an hour.
- The approach is flexible enough to be used for any subject imaginable and compatible enough to allow for the teaching of otherwise complex subjects by moderately prepared volunteer teachers.
- The cost can be $0.00.
- The format can be used by parents with one child, a small group or an auditorium full of kids.
- The subject matter goes right to the heart of why kids are leaving the Church and begins to provide armor for their vulnerable intellects.

There are many more benefits of this approach, not the least of which is that we are taking the best advantage of the short amount of time that we have with these students every week.

Please Return to the Beginning of the Chapter and Take the Post-Test

Where to Start

The First Two Subjects

By including apologetics subjects as a critical piece of the Full Testimony of God, there can be some trepidation as to where to start. If we start philosophically the first subject we address is the *Existence of Truth*. If we start chronologically the *Creation of the Universe from Nothing* might be first. It seems that we would jump right into the deep end of the pool and a long way away from Jesus. I suggest instead that we wade into a heated pool and enjoy the comfortable, familiar water of *Scripture* and *Jesus' Resurrection*.

The two subjects that you should teach right away are the *Reliability of Scripture* and the *Resurrection of Christ*.[22] When your students have a solid evidential justification for these two claims of Christianity, you have made a gigantic leap in securing their faith. These two subjects are foundational to every other subject you will teach.

Hopefully, starting with these subjects will ease some of the anxiety associated with believing you have to start learning the logical arguments for the *Origin of the Universe* or the *Problem of Evil*. You should eventually get to those subjects as part of educating your youth in the proper subject matter, but if Scripture is not reliable and Jesus didn't rise from the dead, then frankly, the rest of it is meaningless.

The challenge for you is that you are not going to address these subjects from a traditional perspective. In typical sermons

---

[22] Both series are may be to download in the Resource section at *www.BraceBarber.com*

on the reliability of Scripture, the pastor will quote 2 Timothy 3:16 (ESV) "*16 All Scripture is breathed out by God and profitable for teaching, for reproof, for correction, and for training in righteousness,*" and 1 Corinthians 2:13 (ESV) "*13 And we impart this in words not taught by human wisdom but taught by the Spirit, interpreting spiritual truths to those who are spiritual.*" There are other favorite passages from within the books of the Bible that claim that the Bible is the Word of God, however, our task is not to repeat what the Bible says about itself, but rather determine if what it says abut itself is true.

Mature Christians can accept the claims of the Bible because we have already come to the conclusion that the Bible is the Word of God. Most of our students have not yet come to that conclusion; therefore, we must approach the teaching by asking the question "Is the Bible the inerrant word of God?" If we were to quote scripture, it would simply be a way of reinforcing the claim, but not as a way of proof.

When you get an email claiming to be from your bank telling you that you need to send them your name and password because of a security update, you don't automatically trust their claim. In fact, you would probably be distrusting of such a claim. You would search for other ways to verify whether or not the email was from your bank and whether or not their warning about the risk to your money was real. Kids are dubious of the claims of the Bible in the same way. They are asking, "Why should I commit my life to Jesus?" It is a fair question and one that these first two subjects cover.

The methods for proving the reliability of Scripture run through several fields of study, including history, archeology, textual analysis and common sense. There are multiple sources for creating one-hour classes that conform to the format that I have described in this book. By picking one component of proof and exploring them individually for four or five weeks, you can comfort your kids with the knowledge that the Bible really is reliable. They will have this knowledge not because the Bible told them so, but because the evidence told them so. They will therefore accept what the Bible says about itself and other things as well.

This standard for proving the reliability of Scripture may seem difficult to achieve, but it is necessary and overwhelmingly rewarding when you succeed. When the Bible is proven reliable as the Word of God, then His purpose for sending the Word becomes a center point around which our faith revolves. Why did God send the word to you? What purpose does he have for you?

The second critical subject to teach is my favorite. I love starting a class with the question, "Is it possible to prove beyond a reasonable doubt that Jesus is resurrected? You wake people up when you put the central tenant of our Christian faith to the test. The vast majority of people believe that they simply have to accept Jesus' resurrection on faith. I won't contest that, but I will exclaim that it is joyous to logically walk someone through to a belief that Jesus really did rise from the dead and ascend into Heaven.

These two subjects lead to exploring God's purpose for sending his Word and his Son. Why did Jesus have to die and what value was there in his resurrection? I believe that after completing these two subjects you will have the setting for treating *Salvation* as an apologetic subject. In the same way that we hold up the other two subjects to question, we should ask, "If God's word is reliable and it tells me that Jesus died and rose again for my sins, then how should I respond?"

If you were getting ready to walk into the desert in the middle of summer, you would take as much water as you could fit into your backpack. Without water, you will die. Everything else you can think of; sunblock, sunglasses, sturdy shoes, light clothes and a hat will ease the burden, but none of them are critical for life.

The subject of the *Reliability of Scripture* is the backpack and *Jesus Resurrection* is the water. No other subject in the Bible even comes close to these two.

Where Does Faith Come In?

In discussing where to start, we must understand from the beginning that by teaching apologetics subjects as part of the Full Testimony of God that the logic and evidence do not create Christians. God's grace creates Christians. In John 6:44 (ESV) Jesus says, *"44 No one can come to me unless the Father who sent me draws him."* Though God draws us, we must make the freewill choice to accept his offer of salvation. Our youth do not understand what that offer of salvation is nor do they believe that it is rational. Our youth are not set up to respond in faith to God's pull. We have told them countless times about the decision for Christ, but they are not prepared to have blind faith.

Faith is necessary in the salvation equation. Rational faith is a short hop, while blind faith is the distance between the two sides of the Grand Canyon. Blind faith is what our youth believe the Church is asking from them. We are telling them that they must *"9 believe in their heart that God raised Jesus from the dead."[23]* They believe that they have to abandon their intellect in order to accept Christ. They believe that they must ignore accepted scientific facts that contradict the Bible in order to be a Christian. Apologetics can never replace faith, but it can turn a canyon into a small ditch.

Rational faith is a short hop, while blind faith is the distance between the two sides of the Grand Canyon

Every time we use the evidence that God has provided for us in support of the gospel, we are filling in the canyon and reducing the burden of faith. Apologetics does not create Christians full of head knowledge and no heart; rather it strengthens the legs of people to ease their step across the ditch into decision for Christ. Their hearts are then filled in Christ.

The Church's dilemma is not between apologetics and the gospel, it is between methods for reducing the canyon that already exists between our kids and their salvation. It is for that reason that I believe that both apologetics and gospel subjects should be taught together as the Full Testimony of God.

---

[23] Romans 10:9 (ESV)

Conclusion

Mark Campbell is a Christian publishing consultant. He and I met at the coffee shop located in a local grocery store to discuss the ideas I had about the ministry God had set spinning in my mind. The location was far from chic and only modestly quiet. A TV on the wall above us played the news, and families periodically traveled the path next to us to the bathroom down the hall. It was as if someone tried to make a quaint coffee shop but ended up with this instead. In spite of the location, our conversation was insightful and Mark's advice that day changed the path of my ministry quite dramatically.

My vision remained the same, *Keep Kids Raised in Christian Homes in the Faith*, but the path to my planned objective got rerouted through the writing of a book. Up until that point, my goal was to spread the message about the way to solve the problem of Christian kids leaving the faith by speaking at Christian Conferences, churches, men's groups and retreats. I had done some writing and was preparing presentation materials and other resources. Mark told me in very clear terms that I had to first write a book that exposed the problem and then walk my audience step-by-step through the solution.

I debated the necessity of creating such a clear path to the solution since the problem was so big and ugly and obvious. I figured that if church leaders were really convinced of the problem and had a general direction of how to solve it, then they would figure out the methods to solve it for themselves.

Mark wisely insisted that I spell out the solution because as I learned through my work, it wasn't as easy as I thought.

I let the new objective bounce around in my thoughts for a few days to decide how I was going to start. In the military, it is nearly a law that if you are going to bring your boss a problem you also have a solution prepared to present. What that meant is that I would have to write two books, not one. One book would be the identification of the problem and the step by step approach to the solution, and the second one would be a custom-designed curriculum that met the criteria of the solution. I started by writing book number two, the custom-designed curriculum – first. That was a mistake.

My mistake is instructive because it parallels the mistake that the Church and curriculum producers have been making for at least a generation. As a strategist, I knew better. I've dealt with countless situations where people and teams, when faced with a challenge jump straight into writing down their plan. The vast majority of people make this mistake, leapfrogging the most important parts of the strategic planning process – clearly defining the solution and war-gaming alternatives. They apply their partial knowledge of the situation to a main course of action and start moving without considering all of the options. This method leaves out the critical steps of clearly defining the characteristics of the solution that they want, analyzing alternative approaches, and the testing of assumptions to determine how they may weaken the plan.

Prior to writing up my solution curriculum, I had done a great deal of research. I had a good idea of what was necessary to solve the problem, and I didn't see anyone else doing it. Though there are wonderful apologetics resources and curriculum out there, the ones I had seen were not condensed enough or at an appropriate level for a Church to widely use. I knew that any solution had to test the students and that it had to include apologetics subjects. As you know, those two characteristics remain at the heart of my solution.

I figured that after I had a refined solution I would guide my justification for the design of the solution to match what I had created. That is important enough to repeat. *I would create a solution and would then justify that solution through my analysis of the problem.* This is the exact method of thinking that major curriculum developers use and it's the reason why student curriculum is so ineffective. I'm not criticizing curriculum producers. They are building on generations of false assumptions that are considered facts.

My mistake was that I had not yet done a thorough analysis of the problem and fully defined the characteristics of a solution that could work with the existing resources. I knew that kids were leaving because they did not believe the Bible or Christian claims to be true. I knew that the Church was merely socializing kids and not measuring their knowledge. I identified the necessity to engage kids' intellect and test their knowledge, and I knew that we needed to give them the ability to evidentially defend the Christian faith.

The book I wrote was titled, *14 Decisions Christian Youth Must Make.* The criteria I used for creating the book are:

1. Subject Matter. Materials provide scientific, historic and philosophical evidence for Christian claims. Any solution without this characteristic was eliminated.
2. Testing/Measuring. Kids are tested on knowledge of scripture and apologetics. Any solution without this characteristic was eliminated.
3. Accessibility. Capability of laymen to lead the study effectively.
4. Compatibility. Compatibility of the program with existing organizational structure, tools and leaders.

14 Decisions meets all of these requirements, but it fails to provide the broad solution that the Church needs. I created a Bible Study curriculum with lessons appropriate for students to read on their own at home and to discuss in class. The subjects roughly follow the, *I Don't Have Enough Faith to be an Atheist*, format from big picture to Christian theology, but I only covered key facts and explanations to focus and shorten the study. Each Chapter starts with the Pre-Test and ends with the Post-Test so that the student gets tested and sees what they have learned. It cannot be a broad Church solution because it is not compatible enough to perform effectively within the one hour a week we have with students. The cure must be able to be administered in one hour per week. I called this last criterion 'Duration' in the solution chapter

5. Duration. The lesson can be effectively taught in one hour.

Because I had jumped ahead in developing my solution before fully analyzing my goal and situation, I totally missed the requirement. Having a solution that was almost good enough was not good enough. I couldn't in good conscience present that solution and then try to justify it. So I went back and produced this analysis and solution.

What you have learned in this book is that the Christian Church is losing the majority of its kids after they graduate from high school. You have learned that the criteria of Subject Matter and Testing/Measuring are critical to any solution that will attempt to solve the problem of kids leaving the faith. You know that I suggest that the Church picks up the slack and solve the problem in the one hour a week that they have the kids. You have also seen that we don't have to wait for anyone or any group to begin the process of strengthening our kids' faith for the future.

Pick a topic, pick an article, pick key facts and create a test. Let them test their knowledge, read the article and test it again. Testing our kids in the key topics that the world attacks before the world attacks will make all of the difference.

There is a great opportunity to succeed through the production of focused curriculum, whether from you or from large publishers. We as Church leaders, as laymen, as parents and as academics can individually and collectively arm our kids to win this battle. We can see kids off into the world that are impacting the world for Christ instead of letting the world impact them. We can prepare our kids to fulfill the Great Commission.

Take some time to look at what and how you are training your youth. How well does your information and method hold up to the criteria that we have identified as being necessary for keeping kids in the faith? Put a check mark next to the criteria you are successfully accomplishing in the table below.

Criteria	Student Curriculum
Subject Matter Full Testimony of God	?
Testing/Measuring	?
Accessibility Laymen Capable	?
Compatibility	?
Duration Within one hour	?

Curing skepticitis is possible by properly and consistently teaching the Full Testimony of God. You have in your hands the key to reversing the loss of kids from the faith. I believe that instead of losing 75% of kids we can retain 75% of kids in the Christian Church. I believe that they will be more enthusiastic and effective evangelists as a result of the work you will do with them using this process.

May God bless your
efforts and our children!

Bruce

About the Author

Brace has walked the halls of West Point, worn out jungle boots in the U.S. Army and toiled with the non-stop to-do lists of companies he has co-founded and built. Over the past 30 years he has had the privilege of experiencing and learning lessons from the challenges, victories and the defeats associated with military service and as a business owner.

He was saved at the age of 27 by God's grace. God presented himself in many apparent ways and countless invisible ways as he drew Brace to him. At West Point there was the straight-laced cadet who maintained his separation from the world in a good way. Brace didn't really know him, but he noticed him. At US Army Ranger School there was the answered prayer for energy when Brace was at the end of his own. Over the years, in quiet conversations with officers that Brace respected for their integrity and clarity of purpose, he was queried about his salvation. Then, after accepting Jesus Christ as his savior there were the countless mercies and revelations that sustained him and his family through the loss of their first child at birth and later the collapse of his first business. God is sufficient.

Brace strives to serve in a simple, transparent manner for the good of those he encounters in a way that brings honor to Christ Jesus. Brace teaches and consults with churches, pastors, groups and conferences about the leadership characteristics and strategy necessary to immediately stem the loss of youth from the faith. His ministry includes high-level teaching to large groups and roll-up-your-sleeves planning and strategy sessions with pastors and small leadership teams.

God has blessed Brace with a wonderful wife and three great kids that he gets to enjoy every day.

Brace is also the author of: *Sun Tzu's Pattern of Power, The Art of War Organized for Decision Making,* (PL Press 2011). *No Excuse Leadership, Leadership Lessons of the U.S. Army's Elite Rangers.* (2004 J. Wiley and Sons) *Ranger School; No Excuse Leadership.* (PL Press 2000) *Bring Back the Blues,* Armor Magazine 1993;

Made in the USA
San Bernardino, CA
05 July 2018